EXPLORING EZEKIEL

AMIR TSARFATI
WITH DR. RICK YOHN

HARVEST PROPHECY
AN IMPRINT OF HARVEST HOUSE PUBLISHERS

Unless otherwise indicated, all Scripture Verses are taken from the New King James Version®. Copyright © 1982 by Thomas Nelson. Used with permission. All rights reserved.

Verses marked ESV are taken from the ESV® Bible (The Holy Bible, English Standard Version®), copyright © 2001 by Crossway, a publishing ministry of Good News Publishers. Used with permission. All rights reserved. The ESV text may not be quoted in any publication made available to the public by a Creative Commons license. The ESV may not be translated in whole or in part into any other language.

Verses marked NLT are taken from the *Holy Bible*, New Living Translation, copyright © 1996, 2004, 2015 by Tyndale House Foundation. Used with permission of Tyndale House Publishers, Inc., Carol Stream, Illinois 60188. All rights reserved.

Verses marked NIV are taken from the Holy Bible, New International Version®, NIV®. Copyright © 1973, 1978, 1984, 2011 by Biblica, Inc.® Used with permission of Zondervan. All rights reserved worldwide. www.zondervan.com. The "NIV" and "New International Version" are trademarks registered in the United States Patent and Trademark Office by Biblica, Inc.®

Cover design by Kyler Dougherty

Original cover design by Faceout Studios

Interior design by KUHN Design Group

For bulk, special sales, or ministry purchases, please call 1-800-547-8979.
Email: CustomerService@hhpbooks.com

This logo is a federally registered trademark of the Hawkins Children's LLC. Harvest House Publishers, Inc., is the exclusive licensee of this trademark.

Exploring Ezekiel
Copyright © 2025 by Amir Tsarfati
Published by Harvest House Publishers
Eugene, Oregon 97408
www.harvesthousepublishers.com

ISBN 978-0-7369-9063-9 (pbk)
ISBN 978-0-7369-9064-6 (eBook)

Library of Congress Control Number: 2025930242

No part of this book may be used or reproduced in any manner for the purpose of training artificial intelligence technologies or systems.

All rights reserved. No part of this publication may be reproduced, stored in a retrieval system, or transmitted in any form or by any means—electronic, mechanical, digital, photocopy, recording, or any other—except for brief quotations in printed reviews, without the prior permission of the publisher.

Printed in the United States of America

25 26 27 28 29 30 31 32 33 / BP / 10 9 8 7 6 5 4 3 2 1

I dedicate this book to my nation, the eternal one, that is subjected to unprecedented hatred yet still stands as living proof of God's faithfulness to His promises, even those given through Ezekiel.

I dedicate this book to my family, friends, and ministry partners. The Lord has taken us through a difficult season, but He is once again throwing open the doors of opportunity to communicate His Word of Truth to the nations.

ACKNOWLEDGMENTS

Thank You, Lord, for Your amazing fidelity, as evidenced in the words of this book. To the faithful, You show Yourself faithful, and to those seeking Your truth, You reveal Yourself in such beautiful and practical ways.

Thank you once again, Dr. Rick Yohn, for your invaluable partnership in the creation of this book. While most have slowed down by your age, you have not. Your example of commitment to the Word and passion for people is refreshing and challenging. Thank you also, Steve Yohn, for your assistance in the writing of this book.

My love and appreciation go out to my wife, Miriam, my four children, and my daughter-in-law for your love and encouragement through the long workdays and the extended absences.

Thank you, Behold Israel team, for your love, support, and dedication—Mike, H.T. and Tara, Gale and Florene, Donalee, Joanne, Nick and Tina, Jason, Abigail, Kayo, Rick, and Steve. Thanks to the CONNECT team for all your hard work. Also, thanks to all your spouses and children, who often sacrifice their family time with you to make possible the further spreading of God's Word.

Thank you to Bob Hawkins, Steve Miller, and the wonderful team at Harvest House for all your hard work in making this book happen.

Finally, thank you so much to the hundreds of thousands of followers, prayer partners, and ministry supporters of Behold Israel. This ministry would not exist without you.

CONTENTS

Who Is This God? 7

1. Experiencing God's Otherness (1–3) 17
2. The Consequences of Failure (3–7) 35
3. Overstaying Your Welcome (8–11) 55
4. Top-Down Sin (12–14) 71
5. Failure Theater (15–19) 85
6. Just How Nasty You Are (20–24) 103
7. Blast Radius (25–28) 123
8. With Frenemies Like These (29–32) 141
9. The Turning of the Page (33–35) 155
10. Rebirth (36–37) 175
11. The Great Ezekiel War (38–39) 197
12. The Return of the King (40–48) 217

Notes 237

WHO IS THIS GOD?

Who am I? The search for identity, purpose, and meaning has become an obsession for many people. It seems that in today's world, there is a need to be noticed, to "be somebody." The social media boom has created a new position of power called an *influencer*, and every young adult—and a huge number of not-so-young ones—dreams of being able to influence the actions of others. Or at least to be listened to. Or maybe just to matter.

Genealogy companies like Ancestry and MyHeritage have exploded because everyone wants to have roots. If we can't find meaning in our daily lives, maybe we can find it in our past. Maybe discovering that we are the direct descendant of someone important can vicariously confer some sort of importance on ourselves. "I'm the eleventh great-granddaughter of King Henry VIII, so…yeah." But that turns into a dead-end road, too, as the March 2025 bankruptcy of 23andMe proved. It may feel great to have important ancestors, but when we come back to real life, we are confronted with the realization that we're still just Ima Jean living in a duplex in Pocatello, Idaho.

Who are you? And, let's add one more question: Why does it

matter? There is one group of people with whom the answer to the first question makes all the difference. In fact, the entire book of Ezekiel answers that question. The people of God had forgotten who they were, or, maybe better put, they had forgotten what being the people of God meant. The Lord was about to change all that. Ezekiel was there to tell them, "This is what is about to happen, and this is why it's about to happen." Jerusalem and the country of Israel were about to be leveled, and their sin was the reason. God had picked Israel out from all the other nations to be His special people. They needed a serious refresher course on the privilege that status held, and the important responsibility that accompanied it.

But Ezekiel's book isn't just about reminding the people who they were. Israel and the world had forgotten their Creator. They had shunted Him to the side like an old-fashioned, has-been God. That was about to change. When the Lord had finished everything He promised in this book, all would know "that He is the Lord."

So You're an Israelite

If you were to ask an everyday Jerusalemite during Ezekiel's era about their identity, they could likely recite to you the Bible stories they had heard from birth. Much like the fantastic epics you'd hear today from many indigenous tribes, Israel's origin tale was a link that bound the people together. But it was not one that most deep down believed or, at the very least, cared about. They were just tales of the ancient times when the great Creator God, who lived on the fiery mountain, thundered out a bunch of rules and brought His people into the land.

It's likely that embellished tales of Noah and the flood and the plagues of Egypt were passed down to the generations around after-dinner campfires. But what about the creation story, Cain killing Abel, the sons of God and the daughters of men, the faithfulness of Abraham, and the trickery of Rebekah? Did people still talk about these things? And how many would have a clue as to the long night when a man wrestled with God? That bout went back and forth until the theophany, God in human form, finally defeated the man, Jacob, by putting his hip out of socket. Yet when God moved to go, He found that Jacob was still hanging on with all his strength.

> He said, "Let Me go, for the day breaks."
> But he said, "I will not let You go unless You bless me!"
> So He said to him, "What is your name?"
> He said, "Jacob."
> And He said, "Your name shall no longer be called
> Jacob, but Israel; for you have struggled with God and
> with men, and have prevailed" (Genesis 32:26-28).

That is the christening story of the nation of Israel. However, most Israelites of Ezekiel's day had likely only heard it occasionally amongst the evening songs of the Babylonian gods Marduk and Bel and Tammuz. And even if they did know the story by heart, it would likely only serve as wishful thinking at best, or biting irony at worst. Israel, the people who have struggled with God and men and have what? Prevailed? Looking around the Promised Land in the era of the Babylonian Empire, the last description anyone would have assigned to the Israelites was that they were a prevailing people.

But as cynical as Israel's name sounded under the given circumstances, it was a God-given name. Therefore, it was accurate. What the people didn't understand was that their sinful actions and those of generations of their ancestors had shifted them from an era of victory back into a time of struggle. In his prophetic book, Ezekiel made it clear that this rebellious battle between the descendants of Jacob and their Creator and Chooser was once again back in full swing. Yes, the Israelites could look to their temple and understand they had a rich history with God. But in their actions, the people were intent on showing that they wanted to reject the rules of the God of Jacob, while still keeping His overall protection. The classic cake-and-eat-it scenario.

The Lord, for His part, regularly reminded the people that no matter what their actions, He wasn't going anywhere. In fact, like a Father disciplining His wayward child, He was determined to stay in it until His progeny's stubborn will was finally broken. He still is today. A time will come in the not-distant future when God's chosen people will once and for all time recognize that He truly is the Lord, a goal found throughout Ezekiel's book.

You Don't Choose Your Father

Of all the people in the world, why did God choose the Jews? There were so many other options out there, so many people groups who were blindly loyal to a god or a nation or an ideology. He could have gone to East Asia with its Hinduism. The Hindu's goal of *moksha*, in which a soul unconsciously merges back into Brahman, the universal god, lessens the importance of the individual here on earth. To their thinking, all descended from the universal soul and to the universal soul all will one day return, so why is there any need for individualism or personal will during this life? Someone without an individual will is very easy to control. Or what about the Islamic militias and jihadists who commit suicide based on false promises and outright lies? You can't find a more dedicated disciple than one who is ready to blow himself up for what he believes to be true. Really, if God was looking for a people who were ready and willing to be His obedient minions, He could have done much better than the people of Israel.

Yet God, in His infinite wisdom, wasn't looking for easy or mindless or blindly obedient when it came to choosing His people. He wanted folks who would give Him a challenge. He needed a nation that would allow Him to show the world who He was through the display of His merciful attributes of grace, long-suffering, and forgiveness.

Israel had the option of living the easy way or the hard way, but God always knew His people would choose the hard way. That was why He spoke the following words to Moses, giving the prophet a final song to teach the people:

> Now therefore, write down this song for yourselves, and teach it to the children of Israel; put it in their mouths, that this song may be a witness for Me against the children of Israel. When I have brought them to the land flowing with milk and honey, of which I swore to their fathers, and they have eaten and filled themselves and grown fat, then they will turn to other gods and serve them; and they will provoke Me and break My covenant. Then it shall be, when many evils and troubles have come upon them, that this song will testify against them as a witness; for it will not be forgotten in the mouths of their descendants, for I know the inclination of their behavior today, even before I have brought them to the land of which I swore to give them (Deuteronomy 31:19-21).

From the very beginning, the people struggled against God. Abraham twice lied about his relationship with his wife. His son Isaac followed suit. Abraham's grandson, Jacob, was a deceiver of the first class. After the people came out of Egypt, it was just a short time before they were worshipping a golden calf. Then there was grumbling and rebellion and stealing devoted things, then more idolatry. The Bible is replete with stories of Israel's failures. Yet God never once let the people's sin change His mind about His choice.

Sure, in the occasional pique of His anger, God was ready to wipe the whole lot out. During the golden calf incident, He said to Moses, "I have seen this people, and indeed it is a stiff-necked people! Now therefore, let Me alone, that My wrath may burn hot against them and I may consume them. And I will make of you a great nation" (Exodus 32:9-10). But even as He threatened to wipe out the nation, He was already planning to rebuild the nation with a member of that same nation. The Jews had been chosen by God, and He would always keep a remnant. Why? Once again, it's because He wants people to know Him.

And it's not just in the past that God proved Himself through the nation of Israel. In chapters 36–39, we'll see that Ezekiel promised a time in which Israel will gather once again as a reestablished nation and prosper greatly economically, although spiritually it will still be distant from its Creator. Once the country is settled and peaceful, it will be attacked by an overwhelming army. But God will supernaturally intervene, protecting His still-rebellious people. The world will recognize this divine involvement, prompting God to once again declare, "Then they shall know that I am the Lord" (Ezekiel 38:23).

Could God have made a better choice than Israel? Using our human peabrains, we might find reasons to say yes. However, because of the perfect wisdom possessed by the All-Knowing, we can be sure that the true answer is undoubtedly no. The Jewish people are not perfect, yet they are the perfect people for God's plan.

A Historical Grounding

"Amir, this is Ezekiel! When are we going to get to the war? I want to read about Gog and Magog and military alliances and all that kind of stuff!" I hear you, and I get it. Chapters 36 and beyond of Ezekiel excite me too. However, we need to lay a foundation. After all, that's what God did. If He thought it best just to jump right into a massive horde marching down from the far north, He wouldn't have included 30-plus chapters of very important prophetic material first. But it is these early prophecies that lay the groundwork for what is to come, because we'll see many similarities as we go between what Jerusalem was facing in Ezekiel's day and what Israel and the rest of the world will have to endure in the end times. So, stick with me. This early business is more important and a whole lot more interesting than you may think.

As I already mentioned, by the time of Ezekiel, Israel's days of wine and roses had passed. After becoming a kingdom under Saul, the nation had flourished through the leadership of Kings David and Solomon. In fact, when Solomon ruled, envoys from countries across the globe journeyed to see the wealth of Jerusalem and to hear the unmatched words of wisdom from its ruler. But, toward the end of that great king's life, cracks were already being seen in Israel's commitment to God, and they were coming from the top down. Although he knew God's law through and through, Solomon either ignored it or felt like parts didn't apply to him. Or at least *a* part didn't apply to him. Through Moses, God said this to the people when they entered the Promised Land:

> You shall make no covenant with [the people] nor show mercy to them. Nor shall you make marriages with them. You shall not give your daughter to their son, nor take their daughter for your son. For they will turn your sons away from following Me, to serve other gods; so the anger of the LORD will be aroused against you and destroy you suddenly (Deuteronomy 7:2-4).

Don't marry those foreign women! They'll turn your hearts toward their gods! Solomon read those words and thought, *Yeah, that's true for all those dummies. But I've got wisdom from God, so I'd never fall into that trap. Now, where are those cuties from Ammon?* The king dove in headfirst to the level that only kings can, and 700 wives and 300 concubines later, it happened exactly as God had said it would.

> For it was so, when Solomon was old, that his wives turned his heart after other gods; and his heart was not

loyal to the LORD his God, as was the heart of his father David. For Solomon went after Ashtoreth the goddess of the Sidonians, and after Milcom the abomination of the Ammonites. Solomon did evil in the sight of the LORD, and did not fully follow the LORD, as did his father David. Then Solomon built a high place for Chemosh the abomination of Moab, on the hill that is east of Jerusalem, and for Molech the abomination of the people of Ammon. And he did likewise for all his foreign wives, who burned incense and sacrificed to their gods (1 Kings 11:4-8).

That began the downward cycle for Israel. With Solomon's son Rehoboam, the kingdom was split in two, with the south calling itself Judah and the north keeping the name of Israel. From that time on, the northern kingdom found itself continuously on the wrong side of God. Not one king followed Him, even up through their destruction and deportation by Assyria in 722 BC.

In the south, it was hit-and-miss with the kings, with more misses than hits. When this book's timeline begins, we are just into the sixth century BC. Ezekiel is a priest who was ripped out of his comfort zone in 597 BC when King Nebuchadnezzar of Babylon had invaded Jerusalem for the second time. This time when the king left, he took 10,000 of its citizens with him to Babylon. Ezekiel was one of these exiles.

For those of you who may be trying to line up the timing of Ezekiel's deportation with that of Daniel, let me lend a hand. Daniel was taken as a teenager to Babylon in the first exile in 605 BC. He was of the royal line and was groomed to serve in the palace. Eight years later, Nebuchadnezzar came back and instituted a much larger deportation. Ezekiel, in his twenties at the time, was just one of the mass of people who made the long journey to start a new life in a foreign land. He settled around Tel-abib, along the Chebar River, about 100 miles or so south of the capital city of Babylon. Four years passed, and he was just starting his life as an exiled priest when God appeared. The Lord called him to be a prophet, and when He did so it was with an amazing flourish, as we'll see in the next chapter.

With the calling of Ezekiel, we now have three prophets at work. Jeremiah is still back in Jerusalem trying to convince the stubborn Israelites to repent and save themselves. It is a futile work. Daniel, likely in his early twenties, has already shown himself as a standout to King Nebuchadnezzar and is on the fast track to Babylonian leadership. Then there's Ezekiel, the common man's prophet. His primary audience was the exiles, but his ministry reached back to Jerusalem and to foreign nations.

Both Ezekiel and Daniel would have known of the great prophet Jeremiah, and Daniel, at least, had probably met him just because of his royal ties. There is no reason to think that an everyday Levite who was too young to be a priest, as was Ezekiel, would have had any interaction with the old prophet. As for Ezekiel and Daniel, undoubtedly Ezekiel would have known of Daniel, who had probably become a hero to all of Israel's exiles in Babylon. Did they ever meet? It's likely, especially once Ezekiel began building his own prophetic reputation. Daniel's position would have afforded him a great amount of independence and movement, and it's hard to imagine him not traveling to Tel-abib or inviting Ezekiel up to the capital city. I wonder what that meeting would have looked like as these two prophets sat down over a cup of tea and some baklava.

CHAPTER 1

EXPERIENCING GOD'S OTHERNESS

EZEKIEL 1–3

The year was 1955 and my writing partner, Rick Yohn, was trying to figure out what to do with his life. Never much of a student, he had somehow allowed himself to get wrangled into teaching at a college group meeting. As he was lying in bed one night, he began thumbing through the lesson material. Out of the blue, the thought came to him, *I'd sure love to teach the Bible the rest of my life.* He bolted upright. Never before had that consideration entered his mind. Now that it had, it felt so right. He didn't know much about a "call to ministry," but from the little he did understand, he figured he may have just had one.

Rick bolted down the stairs and found his mom in the kitchen. He blurted out his news, causing a surprisingly unsurprised smile to spread across her face. "You need to go see Grandma Brown," she said.

It was a short drive, and after being received with a hug, he took a seat across from his great-grandmother's rocking chair. His excitement lengthened his story a bit, and the dear saint listened quietly. When he was done, she said, "Ricky, when my boy was born, I asked

God for a son to go into the ministry. God said, 'No.' Years later, when my first grandchild was born, I asked God for a grandson to go into the ministry. Again, God said, 'No.' Even more years later, when my first great-grandchild was born, I once again asked God for a great-grandson to go into the ministry. Today, God has said, 'Yes.'" Undoubtedly, the decades of prayer from that dear woman, his grandparents on both sides of the family, along with his mother and father, had a strong hand in Dr. Rick's call to service, and that call has produced more than 70 years of ministry.

A call is a powerful experience. When you bring it down to its essence, it is an invitation to the natural to participate in the realm of the supernatural. It is God saying, "My child, I'm going to let you cross the temporal line and do some eternal work." I get that this may sound a little hyperbolic. "Amir, I'm just taking over the second grade Sunday school class because I have a love for kids. It's not like I'm Billy Graham." My response to you, however, is that no, I am not being hyperbolic, and yes, you are like Billy Graham—at least you are to those sticky-fingered little kids as you love them and bless them using the gifts with which God has blessed you.

I'm not denigrating the great Billy Graham in any way. Instead, I am seeking to extol the virtues of your service to the King. Reverend Graham would be the first to tell you that there was nothing special about him. He was just a guy who determined to tirelessly follow the calling given to him. Because of that, he was able to constantly live, serve, and make a powerful impact in the two worlds of the natural and the supernatural.

When Dr. Rick accepted his calling, he also lived that dual residency. I, too, had the same sort of experience when it was clear that serving the Lord was what I wanted to do with my life. As you'll read later in the book, my upbringing was difficult, and I was probably the last kid that most people would expect to stand in front of huge groups of people and talk about God. But that just shows how incredible the Lord is. He took me from a place of despair and gave me hope. He took me from feeling like I had no meaning to giving me a wonderful purpose.

When you say yes to the Holy Spirit's lead, you will find your calling. And, yes, you do have a calling! The apostle Paul made it clear that every believer is gifted and charged by the Holy Spirit "for the profit of all" (1 Corinthians 12:7). He emphasized that point even more to the church in Ephesus, when he wrote that we all have been created to serve God, carrying out the "good works, which God prepared beforehand that we should walk in them" (Ephesians 2:10). Each of us can, and should, carry out our earthly and heavenly dual citizenship every day as we "set [our minds] on things above, not on things on the earth" (Colossians 3:2). Said another way, we live our lives with a ministry mindset, always looking for opportunities to be used by God.

Why am I making such a big deal of this natural/supernatural nature of a call? Because that is exactly what God demonstrated in the first three chapters of Ezekiel. In fact, in a Bible full of dramatic first encounters with God, I don't know that anyone's was more dramatic than Ezekiel's. Paul saw a bright light. Jacob wrestled with a guy. Isaiah had a somewhat less-spectacular throne room experience, if any throne room experience can be considered less spectacular.

Ezekiel, however, was alongside the Chebar River, minding his own beeswax, when suddenly everything went crazy. He saw amazing sights, heard incredible words, and received a divine commissioning. And by the time it was all over, there was no doubt in his mind that the ministry he would be carrying out amongst his fellow natural humans was at the behest of an all-powerful, totally "other," supernatural God.

Setting the Time and Place

This vision is not an allegory! I thought it would be good to get that out right away. It was very important to Ezekiel that his readers knew he wasn't just sitting at his desk making stuff up. He wasn't brainstorming a "this" that could represent a "that" and some "thing" that actually signified some other "thing." The visions he experienced came to him at a certain moment and place in history's timeline. His movements and actions really did take place, as did those of the beings he saw.

It was so important to this prophet that he wouldn't end up in some book entitled *The Allegorical Ethos of the Old Testament Latter Prophets' Myth* that he went overboard time-stamping his book. In at least 13 places within his work, Ezekiel tied his visions and events to specific days in history. The opening words of his book comprise the first example:

> Now it came to pass in the thirtieth year, in the fourth month, on the fifth day of the month, as I was among the captives by the River Chebar, that the heavens were opened and I saw visions of God. On the fifth day of the month, which was in the fifth year of King Jehoiachin's captivity, the word of the LORD came expressly to Ezekiel the priest, the son of Buzi, in the land of the Chaldeans by the River Chebar; and the hand of the LORD was upon him there (Ezekiel 1:1-3).

The fourth month was Tammuz, which was the Babylonian name given to honor the Mesopotamian god of fertility. The Hebrews called it Nisan. The thirtieth year most likely was referring to Ezekiel, marking the age when one in the priestly line could begin his service. Knowing that we would need a more definite temporal anchor than his personal timeline, Ezekiel also told his readers that it was the fifth year of King Jehoiachin's captivity. That was a date that every Israelite could place.

King Jehoiachin, also known in some Bible translations as Coniah, was the second-to-last monarch of Israel. Grandson to the last good king, Josiah, and son of Jehoiakim, he came to power after his father rebelled against Nebuchadnezzar. Some translations have Jehoiachin at age eight and some at 18 when he ascended to the throne. Most likely the latter is true, because three months later, when Nebuchadnezzar exiled him to Babylon, he brought with him his mother and his wives, among others.

As we mentioned earlier, this was the same exile that took Ezekiel and 10,000 others to Babylon. The last king in the Davidic line, Jehoiachin's godless legacy is one that fits the history of the Jewish people. Of this failed monarch, Jeremiah wrote, "Thus says the LORD: 'Write this man down as childless, a man who shall not prosper in his days; for none of his descendants shall prosper, sitting on the throne of David, and ruling anymore in Judah'" (22:30).

Again, most Israelites would recognize the fifth year of King Jehoiachin's reign. However, that particular event doesn't show up on most of our wall calendars today. So, let's interpret up, placing the date as July 31, 593 BC. A real day on a real timeline. Not the timeline Ezekiel and the exiles used, since Pope Gregory XIII was still more than two millennia away from giving us the Gregorian calendar. But, still, an actual day in a format that we modern folks can understand.

As I mentioned in the introduction, Ezekiel had settled in Tel-abib, along the Chebar River. It was a good 100-mile journey north to visit the capital city of Babylon, which was about as close as an exile really wanted to get to the empire's temperamental monarch—just ask Shadrach, Meshach, and Abednego. Ezekiel was an Israelite who lived amongst other Israelites, but we need to remember who those other exiles were. They were IINOs (Israelites in Name Only). They were worshippers of Bel and Marduk and Tammuz and all the other Mesopotamian deities. Sure, they threw the Lord a bone every now and then when they were feeling threatened, but it certainly didn't seem lately like He was obeying their orders like a good little God should. Case in point: They were in Tel-abib, Babylon, instead of Jerusalem. This was still the beginning of the exile, and it was going to take a few decades before we came to the God-fearing refugees who were ready to make the trek back home.

Ezekiel said that at the time of his vision he was "among the captives by the River Chebar" (verse 1). This could simply be referring to his location in the town of Tel-abib, which was near the waterway. However, as the scenario plays out, it becomes evident that to fully take in the grandeur of the events, he needed some wide-open spaces. This would place him alongside the banks of the river when he saw the action take place.

Setting Expectations

What you are about to read has had theologians puzzled and confounded for two-and-a-half millennia. Lucky for you, I'm here to give you all the answers! Oy vavoy, if only! Don't get me wrong. I'm not saying that the visions in these first chapters are arbitrary and open to a wide range of interpretations. Again, this is not an allegory. There are no lines between which we are compelled to read. I'm also not saying that what Ezekiel witnessed was just a huge, supernatural light show with no meaning. Every creature we meet and every wheel that speeds past has an explanation and a purpose. Unfortunately, those explanations and purposes are not always easy to come by.

One of the great blessings of the book of Daniel is that there always seemed to be someone standing near the prophet ready to explain what he was seeing. Daniel saw four great beasts coming out of the sea, one like a lion, one like a bear, one like a leopard, and one unique one with nasty teeth and a bunch of horns (Daniel 7). The prophet had no idea what he was witnessing, but as he looked around, there just happened to be a guy nearby. He asked the man, who turned out to be an angel, for some answers, and the angel replied, "Sure thing. The beasts you are seeing all represent kings." Then he went on to explain the coming kingdoms and the reign of terror of the antichrist.

When Ezekiel looked around for some explanation of the grand display that lit up the sky in front of him, he, too, found someone willing to talk to him. But it wasn't one of God's servants; it was God Himself. And the Lord wasn't bothering with words of explanation. His purpose there was to give a commissioning. So, by the time this vignette ended, Ezekiel had received his marching orders, and we're left wondering what exactly we just beheld. But that's okay. God's primary purpose with Ezekiel's appointing ceremony was different than that of the vision He gave to Daniel. To Daniel, God wanted to give insight into the future. To Ezekiel, God wanted to give a glimpse of Himself.

This brings us back to the "otherness" of God that we touched on in the beginning of this chapter. As we witness the calling of this prophet, there is no doubt that the One who called him is wholly different than we are. He is not a supersized, multi-gifted, humanlike creature, similar to what you typically find in mythology. God is more than just a glorified man, as you find in Mormonism. And His intention, communication, and relationship set Him far beyond the impersonal god-force of Hinduism and Buddhism. In this throne-room theophany, we see a God who is giving us a glimpse behind the supernatural curtain. What we quickly realize, however, is that this is only a peek at the heavenly realm, and, even then, it has been significantly dumbed down so we have somewhat of a chance at grasping it.

Look What the Wind Blew In

If you have ever seen a massive tornado tearing through the central United States, you quite possibly have an idea of what Ezekiel saw coming his way. A huge cloud of Middle Eastern dust, swirling like a whirlwind, rushed toward him as he stood alongside the River Chebar. In the midst of the swirling sand there was a glow, a fire that burst out of the darkness. But that wasn't all that burst out:

> Also from within it came the likeness of four living creatures. And this was their appearance: they had the likeness of a man. Each one had four faces, and each one had four wings. Their legs were straight, and the soles of their feet were like the soles of calves' feet. They sparkled like the color of burnished bronze. The hands of a man were under their wings on their four sides; and each of the four had faces and wings. Their wings touched one another. The creatures did not turn when they went, but each one went straight forward (Ezekiel 1:5-9).

Picture Ezekiel as he witnessed these creatures bursting out of the storm. His jaw must have dropped as the air rushed from his lungs. This was a sight unlike any he had ever seen before.

Now, imagine him later sitting down to try to write a description of his indescribable vision. It's no wonder the words *like* and *likeness* are employed 95 times in his book, 23 in this first chapter alone. The prophet attempted to use natural comparisons to communicate supernatural sights. But as we read through these descriptions, we have to remember that what Ezekiel witnessed was far more amazing and "other" than what his limited vocabulary could define.

As Ezekiel continued his narrative, he attempted to give a more detailed explanation of the four creatures who had appeared:

> As for the likeness of their faces, each had the face of a man; each of the four had the face of a lion on the right side, each of the four had the face of an ox on the left side, and each of the four had the face of an eagle. Thus were their faces. Their wings stretched upward; two wings of each one touched one another, and two covered their bodies. And each one went straight forward; they went

wherever the spirit wanted to go, and they did not turn when they went (Ezekiel 1:10-12).

A man, a lion, an ox, and an eagle. If you've read my book *Revealing Revelation*, you're probably thinking, *Amir, haven't we met this quartet before?* Yes, you most certainly have. In the last book of the Bible, John gave a look into the Lord's throne room, only with a much wider view than our present prophet's. The disciple was ushered before a sea of glass, beyond which was the seat of God. Hovering around the throne "were four living creatures full of eyes in front and in back. The first living creature was like a lion, the second living creature like a calf, the third living creature had a face like a man, and the fourth living creature was like a flying eagle" (Revelation 4:6-7). Just like in Ezekiel, we see a lion, a bovine, a man, and an eagle, all present and accounted for.

What were these beings? It'd be nice to give them a better name than "creature" so that we can picture something more heavenly and beautiful and less black-lagoonish. Good hermeneutics interprets scripture with scripture, so let's briefly jump forward in Ezekiel to when the glory is leaving the temple of God. In the preparation for this tragic event, the prophet saw that "the cherubim were lifted up. This was the living creature I saw by the River Chebar" (10:15). A brief language tip: *im* is the Hebrew signifier for the plural—that is, one cherub, two cherubim.

What Ezekiel, and later John, saw surrounding the throne of God were angels. However, they were very different than the cute, little, diapered Valentine cherubs who live on Hallmark cards. Aren't angels supposed to be beautiful and ethereal, rather than cow-faced or eagle-beaked? Sometimes they are.

Most infamous amongst the cherubim is Lucifer, of whom the Lord said through Ezekiel,

> You were the seal of perfection, full of wisdom and perfect in beauty...You were the anointed cherub who covers; I established you; you were on the holy mountain of God; you walked back and forth in the midst of fiery stones. You were perfect in your ways from the day you were created, till iniquity was found in you...Your heart was lifted up because of your beauty; you corrupted your wisdom for the sake of your splendor; I cast you to the ground, I laid you before kings, that they might gaze at you (Ezekiel 28:12, 14-15, 17).

While beauty is certainly in the eye of the beholder, it is difficult to picture this passage describing a creature that's a man-lion-cow-eagle mash-up.

The confusion surrounding these cherubim increases even more when we read about their circular companions:

> Now as I looked at the living creatures, behold, a wheel was on the earth beside each living creature with its four faces. The appearance of the wheels and their workings was like the color of beryl, and all four had the same likeness. The appearance of their workings was, as it were, a wheel in the middle of a wheel. When they moved, they went toward any one of four directions; they did not turn aside when they went. As for their rims, they were so high they were awesome; and their rims were full of eyes, all around the four of them (Ezekiel 1:15-18).

Enormous eye-covered wheels! I don't know if I should be in awe or feeling a little queasy. This makes me think of Job after God had recited to him just a few of His divine works. He said to the Lord, "I have heard of You by the hearing of the ear, but now my eye sees You. Therefore I abhor myself, and repent in dust and ashes" (Job 42:5-6).

Ezekiel saw, Job heard, and both were thunderstruck by the awesome majesty of the Creator God.

Often, it is easy for us to take God for granted. We can sometimes lose sight of His otherness and let Him slip from all-powerful deity to all-loving pal. To battle against that, we must ensure that we include worship in our daily times with the Lord. We must give Him His due as the Almighty who has created and sustains all things, and as the all-merciful giver of the only salvation and hope that has the power to extend beyond this life.

So, what exactly are these wheels in which are contained the spirits of the four cherubim (Ezekiel 1:20-21)? This is one more area where the veil that separates the natural from the supernatural is particularly thick. It would be nice to know how many types of cherubim there are and how they function. That goes for the seraphim also who are mentioned in Isaiah 6. Are there other types of angels out there as well? Just because the Bible mentions only two doesn't mean that there isn't a myriad of other spiritual beings that God has created for His service. Remember, the Bible includes only what God has determined we need to know, not all that there truly is to know.

And back to the cherubim: What's up with the different faces? I have tried many times to close my eyes and picture these beings, and every time, they seem to show up different. Some say that the four faces represent four aspects of Christ. Others that they are the four Gospel writers, which seems a little out of the chronological order of the Bible. Still others that they are four parts of God's creation, or four qualities of good leadership, or four divisions of the Babylonian zodiac. Again, this is one of those times when it would be very nice to have one of Daniel's guides standing nearby to say, "Oh, the faces? That's easy."

The Lord has told us all we need to know, but He certainly hasn't told us all there is. As Paul wrote, "For now we see in a mirror, dimly, but then face to face. Now I know in part, but then I shall know just as I also am known" (1 Corinthians 13:12). I look forward to the day when the veil is pulled back completely and I can finally know in full. In the meantime, for this book, I am content to avoid speculation, as strong as some of it may be, and keep our focus on the amazing scenario of the big picture.

The Throne of God

As wild and crazy as the cherubim looked with their wheels, they were just the opening act. What Ezekiel was now about to witness is the very vision that all of us look forward to seeing one day in person. Above the heads of the angelic beings was an open space. The NKJV Bible calls it a "firmament," the ESV an "expanse," and the NIV a "vault." The Hebrew word itself, רָקִיעַ (*raqia*), means "to beat out, to spread out," and was used in Genesis 1:6 of the divider God created to separate the waters below from the waters above. Thus, it is something substantial and tangible upon which the seat of God could be set.

> Above the firmament over their heads was the likeness of a throne, in appearance like a sapphire stone; on the likeness of the throne was a likeness with the appearance of a man high above it. Also from the appearance of His waist and upward I saw, as it were, the color of amber with the appearance of fire all around within it; and from the appearance of His waist and downward I saw, as it were, the appearance of fire with brightness all around. Like the appearance of a rainbow in a cloud on a rainy day, so was the appearance of the brightness all around it. This was the appearance of the likeness of the glory of the Lord (Ezekiel 1:26-28).

I have to admit that, as a writer, I feel for Ezekiel. Look at his words—"…the likeness…in appearance like…a likeness with the appearance...as it were...with the appearance..." There were no words adequate to describe the beautiful, majestic otherness of what the prophet was viewing. He knew that he was falling far short of his literary goal, but I've got to give him huge props for doing his best. At least we can get a tiny taste of the wonder that this man witnessed.

When you read Daniel's description of his encounter with the Ancient of Days, there is little doubt that you are in the same throne room as Ezekiel. Each uses different precious stones to try to depict the beauty of the colors surrounding the One on the throne. However, both describe the blazing nature of the throne, with Daniel calling it a "fiery flame, its wheels a burning fire" (Daniel 7:9-10). Combining the two descriptions, one gets the sense of a hallowed God of purity, prepared to judge all that is sinful and unholy. The rainbow Ezekiel spoke of surrounding the throne was later echoed by the apostle John's description of God's inner sanctum, when he wrote, "And He who sat there was like a jasper and a sardius stone in appearance; and there was a rainbow around the throne, in appearance like an emerald" (Revelation 4:3).

After witnessing all the overwhelming and indescribable sights, Ezekiel presented a perfectly descriptive, humble conclusion. "This was the appearance of the likeness of the glory of the Lord. So when I saw it, I fell on my face, and I heard a voice of One speaking" (Ezekiel 1:28-29). The prophet didn't stand around analyzing cherub faces or trying to figure out where all the eyes on the wheels were looking. He didn't get bogged down trying to discern hidden meanings or ancient allusions. When confronted with the absolute otherness of the glory of God, Ezekiel responded the only way possible. He fell on his face.

The Call

There is likely no better place to hear the voice of God than when you are laid out prostrate before Him. No agendas. No distractions. No pride. It is just you, face down, ready to receive the word of the Lord. What would be wonderful to hear when you are in that vulnerable, ready-to-be-used position is God saying, "I am commissioning you to an easy ministry of great success. Through your words people will come to Me, and your service will lead to the revival of many amongst the masses." That, unfortunately, was not what Ezekiel heard when a voice spoke to him from the manifestation of God's glory. He was commanded to get on his feet, a process that was aided by the Holy Spirit entering the prophet. Once Ezekiel was upright, God spoke.

> Son of man, I am sending you to the children of Israel, to a rebellious nation that has rebelled against Me; they and their fathers have transgressed against Me to this very day. For they are impudent and stubborn children. I am sending you to them, and you shall say to them, "Thus says the Lord God." As for them, whether they hear or whether they refuse—for they are a rebellious house—yet they will know that a prophet has been among them (2:3-5).

The tone we get from God's words is, "You're going to talk to them until you're blue in the face, but they're not going to listen to you. They are rebellious children who come from a long line of rebellious children." It's easy to infer from this passage and the rest of chapters 2 and 3 that Ezekiel's mission is doomed to failure. But is it really?

Look again at Ezekiel's calling. He is told to speak to the children of Israel, but nowhere is he told to convert them. Changing minds and lives is beyond Ezekiel's pay grade. The prophet's goal is found in the last line of verse 5—"…yet they will know that a prophet has been among them." That would be the measure of Ezekiel's success. His responsibility was to be faithful and speak the words of the Lord, while leaving the results up to God.

Some may look at my last sentence and see it as a cop-out, but that is far from the truth. It simply means that Ezekiel can focus on what his part of the process is. It's like being a salesman without having to worry about closing the deal. People don't like what you have to say? That's okay. Step on a few toes and turn some people off? So be it. Ezekiel was expected to give his whole life to his calling, but his job was to tell it like it was without having to worry about spinning his message or making it palatable to the masses. The car salesman is everybody's friend, or at least he tries to be. Nobody likes the prophet, especially not those who are enjoying their rebellion.

> You, son of man, do not be afraid of them nor be afraid of their words, though briers and thorns are with you and you dwell among scorpions; do not be afraid of their words or dismayed by their looks, though they are a rebellious house. You shall speak My words to them, whether they hear or whether they refuse, for they are rebellious. But you, son of man, hear what I say to you. Do not be rebellious like that rebellious house; open your mouth and eat what I give you (verses 6-8).

These are not a people who are ready to hear what God wants to say to them. In Ezekiel's book, the word "rebellious" is used 17 times, almost always to describe Israel. Four of these occurrences are in these three verses alone. But God told his prophet to not be afraid of the people. Ezekiel would be speaking God's words. His job was to talk, and the Lord would take care of the rest. But from where would the prophet receive his divine message?

A Tasty Scroll

Let's reorient ourselves in the scene. Ezekiel was down by the Chebar River. Suddenly, a huge whirlwind began to roll toward him, and out of the maelstrom came four amazingly other-looking cherubim along with their four eye-filled wheels. Then, above the cherubim, a throne appeared with an enormous figure on it. Ezekiel knew right away that this was a manifestation of the glory of the Lord. The soon-to-be prophet dropped to the ground, but was hefted back up to his feet by an infusion of the Holy Spirit. Then the figure on the throne told Ezekiel that He was sending him to prophesy to his own people, who would likely not listen to him because of their rebelliousness.

Ezekiel had received a vision of the Lord and his calling from the Lord. Now he was about to receive into himself the Lord's message.

> Now when I looked, there was a hand stretched out to me; and behold, a scroll of a book was in it. Then He spread it before me; and there was writing on the inside and on the outside, and written on it were lamentations and mourning and woe. Moreover He said to me, "Son of man, eat what you find; eat this scroll, and go, speak to the house of Israel" (Ezekiel 2:9–3:1).

The prophet was quick to obey, taking the scroll and ingesting it. Despite the words on the scroll being extremely sour, the flavor was "like honey in sweetness" (3:3). It's possible that this is because God's justice seems harsh to the unrighteous, but is pure and proper to the righteous.

This is one of three biblical examples of God's Word being eaten by His spokesmen. In Revelation, John is told by a heavenly voice to eat a little book held by a massive angel.

> I went to the angel and said to him, "Give me the little book." And he said to me, "Take and eat it; and it will make your stomach bitter, but it will be as sweet as honey in your mouth." Then I took the little book out of the

angel's hand and ate it, and it was as sweet as honey in my mouth. But when I had eaten it, my stomach became bitter. And he said to me, "You must prophesy again about many peoples, nations, tongues, and kings" (Revelation 10:9-11).

The angel's words indicated that it was a book of judgment against the unrighteous still alive at that point in the tribulation. Unlike Ezekiel's scroll, John's book did not sit well with his insides.

There was one more incident of a prophet eating the words of God, and it happened not too many years before Ezekiel's consumption of a scroll. Jeremiah had also been tasked to fruitlessly preach to the rebellious people of Israel. Unfortunately for him, he had to do so from Jerusalem, with its idolatrous leadership and culture, and the eventual deprivation and destruction brought about by the Babylonian siege and conquest. At one moment, when Jeremiah was bemoaning the weight of the task God had given to him, he said, "Your words were found, and I ate them, and Your word was to me the joy and rejoicing of my heart; for I am called by Your name, O Lord God of hosts" (Jeremiah 15:16). We don't know what words God had written on what was likely another scroll, but when Jeremiah swallowed it, they gave him what he needed to keep pushing through with the enormous task given to him.

This eating of the Word of God is a poignant activity. It emphasizes to the prophets that the message they were carrying to the masses was from Him. It was a tactile experience to point out what they already knew mentally. For each of them, when the pushback may have been at its greatest, they had that scroll-swallowing moment to remind themselves that these difficult words they were speaking were from God and were 100 percent accurate.

After Ezekiel ate the scroll, God affirmed the greatness and importance of the task ahead of him. The Lord also reminded His new prophet that He had equipped him with everything needed to accomplish his assignment, even emphasizing that as hard as the Israelites' heads were, God had made Ezekiel's head even harder.

When the Lord finished speaking, another powerful voice cried out, "Blessed is the glory of the Lord from His place!" (3:12). As the praise was called out, Ezekiel was carried away by the Holy Spirit. The rustling of the cherubs' wings, the whirring of the wheels, and a deafening noise of some sort accompanied his departure. As the Spirit carried him, Ezekiel was greatly disturbed, which is completely understandable. What he had just witnessed would shake up anyone. Add to that the life-altering commission he had received to be a prophet—a calling that rarely ended well for the callee.

Was this transportation back to the River Chebar a physical transfer, like Philip later experienced with the Ethiopian eunuch (Acts 8:39)? Or was this merely a vision, during which Ezekiel had never physically moved from his location? We can't know for sure, but because the passage never indicates Ezekiel's physical departure from the riverside, I would lean toward him having remained there in a visionary state.

Once Ezekiel returned to his fellow exiles, he sat greatly distressed for seven days. It was gracious of God to give him that time to recover, because when that week was over, it was time to hit the ground running.

CHAPTER 2

THE CONSEQUENCES OF FAILURE

EZEKIEL 3–7

When people begin a new job, they usually do so in one of two ways. There are those who slide in quietly and set to work. Then there are those who barrel in with a bang. When Donald Trump began his nonconsecutive second term as president in 2025, he immediately made it clear that there was a new sheriff in town. Programs were cut. People were sacked. Elon Musk fired up his Department of Governmental Efficiency mower to trim the weeds of wild spending down to a nice, smooth lawn.

But it wasn't just America that felt the Trump blast. The Gulf of Mexico became the Gulf of America; Israel heard that Gaza was destined to become the next Riviera; and Canada was invited to become the fifty-first or fifty-second state, depending on whether they beat Greenland to the punch. Even Trump's vice president, J.D. Vance, went scorched earth when he visited Europe, using an international security conference to harshly criticize the Western nations for their unwarranted censorship and erosion of democracy. His words caused such a diplomatic earthquake that they moved the chair of the conference to tears in his closing speech. And it takes a lot to make a stoic German cry.

When God called Ezekiel into the role of a prophet, He was determined to do it with a bang. There would be no subtleties, no confusing messages. To any of the exiles in Babylon who may have been feeling relieved that at least they didn't have to listen to Jeremiah's doom and gloom prophecies anymore, God said, "Yeah? Well, just wait until you get a glimpse of the new guy!"

Ezekiel the Watchman (3:16-21)

Before Ezekiel could effectively present God's expectations before the people, he needed to understand God's expectations of himself. Once the prophet had recovered from the shock of his calling, the Lord gave him a title. "Son of man, I have made you a watchman for the house of Israel" (Ezekiel 3:17). The watchman was the person tasked with sentry duty. It was an extremely important job because he stood guard as the population slept through the night. If the enemy approached, his job was to sound the alarm. If he fooled around or dozed while on duty, it could potentially cost the lives of all who were under his care. Thus, the watchman knew that shirking his duty could mean a court martial, prison time, and even his life.

Israel was spiritually asleep. The people worshipped the gods of the nations around them, sacrificing to idols and offering up their children in the fire. God was disgusted by this somnolence to the truth. He needed His people to wake up to their sin and the consequences that were approaching as a result. Repentance was an immediate necessity for Jerusalem to stand a chance of survival. Ezekiel was not the first watchman God had sent, according to Jeremiah. "Also, I set watchmen over [Judah], saying, 'Listen to the sound of the trumpet!' But they said, 'We will not listen'" (Jeremiah 6:17). Now that a mass deportation had taken place, maybe the remnant would listen to a voice from the exile. Could a prophet from captivity shake those left in the holy city to repentance?

Probably not. But, as we mentioned earlier, success for Ezekiel is in the obedience, not in the results. The Lord said to him:

> When I say to the wicked, "You shall surely die," and you give him no warning, nor speak to warn the wicked from his wicked way, to save his life, that same wicked man shall die in his iniquity; but his blood I will require at your hand. Yet, if you warn the wicked, and he does not turn from his wickedness, nor from his wicked way, he shall die in his iniquity; but you have delivered your soul (Ezekiel 3:18-19).

God then emphasizes this point using the example of a righteous person turning to iniquity. Once again, Ezekiel has not the option, but the responsibility, to call the person out for their sin. To do less would be to fail in his role as a watchman. Would his words turn around the intended spiritual target? Maybe, maybe not. But without the words of the watchman, the odds of "maybe not" are infinitely greater.

This role of watchman was key to who Ezekiel was as a prophet. In fact, it's a role so nice, God gave it twice. Thirty chapters from now, we will read the words, "So you, son of man: I have made you a watchman for the house of Israel; therefore you shall hear a word from My mouth and warn them for Me" (33:7). That is the point in the book when God turned His eyes back on the nation of Israel, predicting their fall and their ultimate destruction by Babylon. One last time, Ezekiel and Jeremiah and any remaining unnamed prophets God had called to be watchmen would lift their voices and plead for the repentance of Israel. But their cries would fall on deaf ears.

A Divine Message

With the personal and national stakes so high, Ezekiel's stress level must have shot up. How would he know what to say and when to say it? What if God gave him a message and he misunderstood it? What if he accidentally wrote off a divine vision as a bad dream? As always, there was no need for the new prophet to worry, an assurance that God now gave to him.

At the Lord's behest, Ezekiel went out to the river again, and there beheld the glory of God. As we saw earlier, what is the customary reaction when seeing the glory of God? You lose all muscle control and fall on your face, which is what Ezekiel proceeded to do. And, as we saw in Ezekiel 2:2, it was the Spirit entering the prophet that gave him the strength to return to his feet. In other words, it was the *Spirit* of God who gave him the power to stand before the *glory* of God.

There is a difference, though, between the vision Ezekiel received now and what we saw in chapter 2. Then, the Spirit lifted up Ezekiel so that he could hear the words of the One on the throne. This time, as the Spirit filled him and he stood before the Lord, it was the Holy Spirit Himself who spoke with the prophet. As we read the words He said, this distinction makes sense:

> The Spirit entered me and set me on my feet, and spoke with me and said to me: "Go, shut yourself inside your house. And you, O son of man, surely they will put ropes on you and bind you with them, so that you cannot go out among them. I will make your tongue cling to the roof of your mouth, so that you shall be mute and not be one to rebuke them, for they are a rebellious house. But when I speak with you, I will open your mouth, and you shall say to them, 'Thus says the Lord God.' He who hears, let him hear; and he who refuses, let him refuse; for they are a rebellious house" (3:24-27).

First, the Spirit told Ezekiel to go into his house and shut the door. Then, you get these odd verses about being tied up and making Ezekiel's tongue stick to the roof of his mouth. There is a lot of speculation that maybe the people bound Ezekiel to keep him from bothering them, or that God took away Ezekiel's ability to speak except when he was prophesying. If either of those are true, I would think the second to be more likely than the first. But it's quite possible that both were figures of speech. As Dr. Tony Evans wrote:

> There doesn't seem to be any evidence that [the binding of Ezekiel] was a physical threat: instead, God intended to create an object lesson for the people about their refusal to hear Ezekiel's message. The same can be said for Ezekiel's tongue sticking to the roof of his mouth (3:26). It suggests that he wouldn't have anything to say to the rebellious Israelites unless it was the message God had given him.[1]

Whether Ezekiel was permanently made dumb unless the Holy Spirit loosened his tongue or he just remained in his house without speaking to outside folks unless the Lord gave him a message, we can't say with absolute certainty. What is obvious is that the prophet was not much of a socialite. The people would shun Ezekiel, and God was content with having him shunned, because that meant that when he finally stepped out and started speaking, the people would likely listen. The importance of the prophet's words derived from the source of his words. The Holy Spirit would put the message of the Lord God into Ezekiel's mouth for the people to hear.

Does this sound familiar to you? It certainly had me reaching for the Gospels, because there is a ring of the Messiah's voice in these words. In the presence of a large crowd, Jesus warned His disciples of dire times ahead. Still, He gave them this encouragement: "Now when they bring you to the synagogues and magistrates and authorities, do not worry about how or what you should answer, or what you should say. For the Holy Spirit will teach you in that very hour what you ought to say" (Luke 12:11-12). Later, just hours before He was betrayed, Jesus told His disciples:

> I still have many things to say to you, but you cannot bear them now. However, when He, the Spirit of truth, has come, He will guide you into all truth; for He will not speak on His own authority, but whatever He hears He will speak; and He will tell you things to come. He will glorify Me, for He will take of what is Mine and declare it to you. All things that the Father has are Mine. Therefore I said that He will take of Mine and declare it to you (John 16:12-15).

This is a key role of the Holy Spirit. He is the conduit that transfers the words of the Father and the Son into our minds, then out of our mouths to the ears of the world. This was true in the Old Testament. This was true during the time of the New Testament. And it is true now. When we take the chance to share our faith, we are not alone. The Holy Spirit is there speaking to us and through us.

If we risk a gospel presentation, are we guaranteed success? Yes and no. Yes in that we will have fulfilled our role as watchmen, and that is all God is asking for. No in that there is always the possibility that our words will fall on deaf ears. As the Holy Spirit told Ezekiel, "He who hears, let him hear; and he who refuses, let him refuse; for they are a rebellious house" (Ezekiel 3:27).

Show and Tell (4–5)

I'm a firm believer in communicating truth in various ways. That is why I go on speaking tours, present video teachings, and write books. When I communicate through books, I do so using both fiction and nonfiction. Different people learn different ways. So, whether it is in person or online, in a teaching book or woven through a thrilling story, I want to offer as many handles as possible for people to take hold of the truth.

In the history of the prophets, there were many who simply stood before the people and spoke God's words, as well as many others who added a demonstration to their proclamations. Ezekiel was of both the "show" and "tell" school of prophecy. And his first assignments definitely leaned more toward the "show."

Sign One: A Clay Tablet

God called Ezekiel to perform a number of signs, each designed to demonstrate the terrible fate that was to befall the city of Jerusalem. The first sign would challenge the prophet's artistic abilities.

> You also, son of man, take a clay tablet and lay it before you, and portray on it a city, Jerusalem. Lay siege against it, build a siege wall against it, and heap up a mound against it; set camps against it also, and place battering rams against it all around (4:1-2).

I love trying to picture this scene. It reminds me of a scaled-down version of war reenactors who create a battlescape in their basement of Napoleon at Waterloo, or the Siege of Orléans, or the Battle of Gettysburg. Ezekiel's panorama began with a clay tablet upon which he had drawn Jerusalem. Surrounding the brick would be the tiny tents of the Babylonian army, and piled against the clay surface would be built a small siege wall for the soldiers to climb up. At the etched-in gates would be mini-battering rams trying to break through the flat surface.

Those who came to witness this drama-in-miniature performed by Ezekiel would know instantly what the scene depicted. "Where is

God in this?" they would wonder. "Isn't He supposed to protect His people?" Ezekiel would answer their question, once again not with words, but with actions. God tasked the prophet to now depict His role by placing "an iron plate" between himself and the city. Even if the Lord had wanted to intervene, the sin of the people and His own sense of justice would act as "an iron wall" barring Him from saving the city (verse 3).

Sign Two: Ezekiel Lying Down

When you first read of this next sign, it may not appear too bad. "You know, I work pretty hard. I could do with a nice, long vacation off my feet." But then you come across the details and it loses much of its luster. "Wait—430 days stretched out on the hard ground just staring at my little clay siege? What about my adjustable bed? What about my Netflix?" Suddenly, 430 days sounds less like a vacation and more like a sentence.

But that is what Ezekiel was called to:

> Lie also on your left side, and lay the iniquity of the house of Israel upon it. According to the number of the days that you lie on it, you shall bear their iniquity. For I have laid on you the years of their iniquity, according to the number of the days, three hundred and ninety days; so you shall bear the iniquity of the house of Israel. And when you have completed them, lie again on your right side; then you shall bear the iniquity of the house of Judah forty days. I have laid on you a day for each year (verses 4-6).

Three-hundred-and-ninety days for the northern kingdom and 40 days for the south. Each day was to represent a year of sin perpetrated by each kingdom. "Amir, I get the siege and days representing years, but what do the 390 and the 40 mean?" Oy, I was hoping you wouldn't ask. This is another of those passages that have commentators jousting and seminary theologians arm-wrestling in the staff lounge. Some see these numbers as referring to the past, but some say they are in the future. Some see these as literal years, while others believe they are symbolic of something else. After reading many different options, I tend to go with what my friend Dr. Charlie Dyer wrote:

> Perhaps the best solution is to see the numbers as referring to the past. The 390 days corresponded to "the years of their sin" (v. 5), not the years of their chastisement. Yet no specific years can be determined with any certainty. But while the details are unclear, the message is obvious—Babylon would lay siege to Jerusalem because of her sin, and in some way the length of the siege would correspond to the years of her sin.[2]

Once again, rather than get bogged down in the minutiae, we'll go with what is evident. Israel had sinned, and God would punish the people for their sin. This is pure cause and effect.

While Ezekiel was lying down, the Lord told him, "Surely I will restrain you so that you cannot turn from one side to another till you have ended the days of your siege" (verse 8). Some have interpreted this as Ezekiel having people tie him up each day so that he couldn't move. But the words "I will restrain you" seem too direct for outside involvement. A more plausible explanation is that each day when Ezekiel assumed his position alongside the siege display, God would lock him into place. The only movement he would be allowed was the waving of his arm as he was prophesying against Israel.

What was God showing with this demonstration? It becomes obvious when we remember the iron plate standing between the prophet and the city. It takes me to the time during Jesus' final week, when He mourned, "O Jerusalem, Jerusalem, the one who kills the prophets and stones those who are sent to her! How often I wanted to gather your children together, as a hen gathers her chicks under her wings, but you were not willing!" (Matthew 23:37). God was waiting for His people to turn back to Him. He wanted to bless them and protect them, but their sin put up an iron wall. It's tragic to picture Ezekiel lying so close but so far from the mini-city, knowing that God was ready to rescue beloved Jerusalem, but His people were too rebellious to ask.

Sign Three: Foul Famine Food

Over the years, I have seen numerous biblically related diets pop up. The Daniel Diet, the Hallelujah Diet, the Maker's Diet, and others promising you health by eating food God's way. Interestingly, though, I've never seen a book called *The Ezekiel Diet*. There's probably a good reason for that.

> "Also take for yourself wheat, barley, beans, lentils, millet, and spelt; put them into one vessel, and make bread of them for yourself. During the number of days that you lie on your side, three hundred and ninety days, you shall eat it. And your food which you eat shall be by weight, twenty shekels a day; from time to time you shall eat it. You shall also drink water by measure, one-sixth of a hin; from time to time you shall drink. And you shall eat it as barley cakes; and bake it using fuel of human waste in their sight." Then the LORD said, "So shall the children of Israel eat their defiled bread among the Gentiles, where I will drive them" (Ezekiel 4:9-13).

To drink, there is only water. To eat, there is bread cooked on human excrement. I can guarantee you that I would lose a ton of weight if that were my diet. The interesting thing about this third sign is that it is the first one that looks primarily to the time after the fall of Jerusalem. The famine in Jerusalem during the siege will be horrible, but it's not going to get much better for the survivors after the destruction of the great city. The last sentence in the passage above makes it clear that Ezekiel will depict the diet of those who are driven away from the remains of Jerusalem into the land of the Gentiles.

Obviously, this was not the way that the exiles of Ezekiel's deportation were living. They certainly weren't in the lap of luxury, but the prophet wouldn't have had the same reaction if he was used to cooking his dinner using his own refuse. This is likely referring to the rebellious remnant still among Jerusalem's ruins after the siege and the final deportation. Those people ignored God's demand that they remain in the land, and they fled to Egypt. The long journey would have been extremely difficult with most everything having been wiped out during the invasion. The supplies they departed with would have been few, and once they made it to Egypt, their circumstances wouldn't have gotten better. Pharaoh's once-great empire had also been devastated by Babylon and was on its last legs.

When you keep your back turned to God, there is no point when you will experience a genuine turnaround in your circumstances. There will always be something remaining to bring you down. The remnant may have been free from the murderous siege by Babylon, but they were still left with poverty, famine, and no home. Worst of all, they had no hope once their shabby lives were over. That same truth is faced by everyone in this world who rejects the Messiah, no matter their station in this life.

In the assigning of this task, there is a brief, interesting interaction between Ezekiel and God. When the Lord gives him his assignment, the prophet bristles. "Ah, Lord GOD! Indeed I have never defiled myself from my youth till now; I have never eaten what died of itself or was torn by beasts, nor has abominable flesh ever come into my mouth" (verse 14). Nowhere in the Mosaic law is cooking with human waste prohibited, but it was certainly not acceptable, as evidenced by God calling the food "defiled" in the previous verse.

If Ezekiel had eaten the bread as originally commanded by God, would he have been breaking the law? No. James wrote, "Let no one say when he is tempted, 'I am tempted by God'; for God cannot be tempted by evil, nor does He Himself tempt anyone" (James 1:13). However, God understood Ezekiel's desire to remain holy before Him, and He knew this would have put a strain on his conscience. So He allowed his prophet to upgrade his cooking materials to cow dung—the word *upgrade* being a relative term.

Sign Four: A Close Shave

The fourth sign in this quartet continues the heartbreaking theme. Using the hairs of his head and face, Ezekiel demonstrated the death that would come upon the people.

> You, son of man, take a sharp sword, take it as a barber's razor, and pass it over your head and your beard; then take scales to weigh and divide the hair. You shall burn with fire one-third in the midst of the city, when the days of the siege are finished; then you shall take one-third and strike around it with the sword, and one-third you shall scatter in the wind: I will draw out a sword after them. You shall also take a small number of them and bind them in the edge of your garment. Then take some of them again and throw them into the midst of the fire, and burn them in the fire. From there a fire will go out into all the house of Israel (Ezekiel 5:1-4).

Strange behavior, to be sure. But before those watching this divine demonstration by Ezekiel were to receive the explanation of his actions, they were destined to hear the reason for it being done. And it was harsh. The words of the Lord spoken through the prophet made it clear that it was the sins of the people that brought this about. He warned them, He punished them, He tried to set them straight, but they continued to sin to such an extent that they outdid the nations around them in depravity.

This leads to the key verse in this passage, in which the Lord God declared to the children of Israel, "Indeed I, even I, am against you and will execute judgments in your midst in the sight of the nations" (verse 8). Imagine the all-powerful God of all creation is against you. How do you stand up against that? This tragic statement was followed by one of the harshest, most heartbreaking litanies of judgment that the Lord ever uttered against His people.

It is in this catalog of catastrophe that we find the meaning behind the hair. The Lord said, "One-third of you shall die of the pestilence, and be consumed with famine in your midst; and one-third shall fall by the sword all around you; and I will scatter another third to all the winds, and I will draw out a sword after them" (verse 12). Two-thirds will be destroyed, while one-third will flee Jerusalem with a sword chasing behind them.

This takes me to the words of another prophet who comes only a few decades after Ezekiel. Speaking of the time during the tribulation when the antichrist will remove his "man of peace" mask, revealing his true nature, Zechariah wrote:

> "It shall come to pass in all the land,"
>   says the Lord,
> "That two-thirds in it shall be cut off and die,
>   but one-third shall be left in it:
>   I will bring the one-third through the fire,
>   will refine them as silver is refined,
>   and test them as gold is tested.
>   They will call on My name,

and I will answer them.
I will say, 'This is My people';
And each one will say, 'The LORD *is* my God'" (13:8-9).

As in the days of Ezekiel, two-thirds of all Jews will be wiped out, while the remaining third flees Jerusalem. However, there is a huge difference between the two accounts regarding the fate of this final third. In Ezekiel, the survivors continue in their rebellion, eventually escaping to Egypt. There, they all meet their ends when Babylon comes to destroy Pharaoh's empire.

A very different fate awaits the remnant third of Zechariah. They will escape the sword, fleeing, according to the vision given to the apostle John, "into the wilderness to her place, where she is nourished for a time and times and half a time, from the presence of the serpent" (Revelation 12:14). At the end of that final three-and-a-half years of Jacob's trouble, the Messiah will return, these remaining Jews will see the One they pierced, they will each receive Him as their personal Lord and Savior, "and so all Israel will be saved" (Romans 11:26).

Death and the Remnant (6)

Throughout Israel's history, God showed His love for His people. And there were periods of time when they showed their love back through worship and obedience. But those days of reciprocal love were few and far between. Before you knew it, the people were back to worshipping the gods of the nations around them.

It's no wonder the people of Israel grieved God to such an extent. He was the perfect Husband whose wife still went out catting at night. Then she started going out during the day too. Finally, she just stayed out. His anger was understandable, and His discipline was essential if there was to be any hope for His wayward spouse. So, because of His love for His people, He brought what was necessary to give the nation a chance of getting right with Him again.

Now the word of the LORD came to me, saying: "Son of man, set your face toward the mountains of Israel, and prophesy against them, and say, 'O mountains of Israel, hear the word of the Lord GOD! Thus says the Lord GOD to the mountains, to the hills, to the ravines, and to the valleys: "Indeed I, even I, will bring a sword against you, and I will destroy your high places. Then your altars shall be desolate, your incense altars shall be broken, and I will cast down your slain men before your idols. And I will lay the corpses of the children of Israel before their idols, and I will scatter your bones all around your altars. In all your dwelling places the cities shall be laid waste, and the high places shall be desolate, so that your altars may be laid waste and made desolate, your idols may be broken and made to cease, your incense altars may be cut down, and your works may be abolished. The slain shall fall in your midst, and you shall know that I am the LORD"'" (Ezekiel 6:1-7).

Harsh words, difficult to even read. But these people had forgotten who God truly was. They treated Him like a genie in a bottle. When He wasn't needed to do some great work, He was capped off and tucked away on a bookshelf where He couldn't bother anyone with His "do this and don't do that." But God will not be tucked away. He will not be mocked through apathy and disinterest, then expected to perform at the drop of a hat (Galatians 6:7). This harsh prophecy is one more reminder to the people that He is God and there is no other (Isaiah 45:5). When the ramifications of God's severe promise come to pass, any survivors, as well as those who perish, will know that He is the Lord.

Still, the words promise so much death and destruction. It's hard to balance this sometimes with the truth that God is loving. However, this was a lost generation. Like in the days of Noah, God knew when folks were too far gone to bring them back. But also like in the days of Noah, He didn't wipe out everyone. As was also true in the time of Lot, there were a handful who were worth preserving. Even among the ashes a few sparks still glowed with the love of the Lord, and He had a plan for them.

> Yet I will leave a remnant, so that you may have some who escape the sword among the nations, when you are scattered through the countries. Then those of you who escape will remember Me among the nations where they are carried captive, because I was crushed by their adulterous heart which has departed from Me, and by their eyes which play the harlot after their idols; they will loathe themselves for the evils which they committed in all their abominations. And they shall know that I am the LORD; I have not said in vain that I would bring this calamity upon them (Ezekiel 6:8-10).

Remember when Ezekiel was illustrating God's judgment with his hair. One-third he burned, one-third he cut, and one-third he scattered. But there were still a few hairs the Lord told Him to hold back. "You shall also take a small number of them and bind them in the edge of your garment" (5:3). That is the remnant He is now talking about. They will be God's living witnesses to the carnage and to its reason. The Lord made a "blessing for obedience, curse for disobedience" deal with Israel. Israel welched on their end of the bargain, so God carried out His. As verse 10 above essentially says, "I told you this would happen, and now they know that I am the one and only Lord who could bring it about."

Four times in this chapter, God emphasized that point. He was not bringing destruction to be mean or because He was sinfully vengeful.

Their adulterous hearts deeply wounded Him, but He wasn't striking back out of anger. The only way to live a worthwhile and purposeful existence in this life and to have the assurance of a glorious eternity after our time is over is to follow and serve the one true God. While "they shall know that I am the Lord" can have an ominous tone about it, the purpose behind the words speaks of grace, forgiveness, and mercy. Only when we recognize that God exists and that He is our Lord can we believe in Him and love Him and serve Him.

The people in Jerusalem had their opportunity to follow God. They rejected Him. Now, they will be used as an object lesson to prove to all who come later that God is not to be trifled with and that He always keeps His promises.

Song of Sorrows (7)

Let me first say that the writing in Ezekiel 7 is brilliant. The wording is exquisite, but the pacing is what really makes it work. Short phrases, one after the other. The reader feels the quick passing of time. Judgment is at the gates. Destruction has arrived.

> A disaster, a singular disaster;
> behold, it has come!
> An end has come,
> the end has come;
> it has dawned for you;
> behold, it has come! (7:5-6).

Reading those words, it's not hard to picture yourself running through the streets as the enemy bursts through the gates. Horns blare, metal clangs against metal, screams surround you. As you flee down the crowded street, you see people taken down by the sword and the spear and you are dreading the moment the steel finds you. Then you feel it—the hard punch of a blade through your skin. You stumble to the ground in an awkward heap. As your lifeblood drains from you, any peace you may have found is drowned out by the frenzy of violence in the surrounding melee.

These were real people dying one by one at the hands of an invading army. Each life ended one at a time, souls leaving bodies to meet their eternal fate. Whichever direction these souls went, each person would have only themselves to blame.

In this beautiful, tragic song, that transactional characteristic is a point that God is making to the readers. This was not due to the Lord's whim. He was not being malicious. It was a product of the people's choices. Five times in this chapter, we find a combination resembling "according to your ways" and "I will repay" (verses 3, 4, 8, 9, 27). It's the old adage, "If you can't do the time, then don't do the crime." They had fallen deeply into idolatry, and now there was a price they had to pay.

End of an Era (7)

What was taking place in Jerusalem wasn't simply the end of a population, it was the end of the kingdom era. This is made clear throughout this song with words like "disaster" and "destruction," and phrases like "doom has come" and "the end has come." What began with Saul was completed with Zedekiah. When the exiles returned, they would do so as a vassal state of the Persian Empire. Their allegiance would pass to the Greeks, then the Egyptians, then back and forth between the two a few more times, until the Romans came in. Caesar would be their king for many years until the Jews of the land bore the consequences of their rebellion in the first century and the early second century and were mostly dispersed. It was a hard but just punishment for an adulterous nation. As Ezekiel wrote:

> The king will mourn, the prince will be clothed with desolation, and the hands of the common people will

tremble. I will do to them according to their way, and according to what they deserve I will judge them; then they shall know that I am the LORD! (7:27).

The end of the kingdom of Israel—as promised centuries earlier by an all-powerful God of justice—is proof that He is the Lord. What's missing from this song is the promise found in many other places in Ezekiel that the kingdom that was destroyed because of God's holiness and justice will be reborn as a result of His mercy, grace, and love. And sitting on the throne of that resurrected kingdom will be our resurrected Savior, Jesus. As the angel promised Jesus' mother, Mary:

> He will be great, and will be called the Son of the Highest; and the Lord God will give Him the throne of His father David. And He will reign over the house of Jacob forever, and of His kingdom there will be no end (Luke 1:32-33).

What the hearers of Ezekiel's prophecy could only understand as a full stop to the once-great nation of Israel, we, as possessors of the fullness of the Scriptures, can recognize as a necessary comma in the complete statement of God's eternal kingdom.

So when we read the story of Ezekiel, we do so with heavy hearts, knowing that so many men, women, and children were having their sinful mortal lives brought to an end, only to have their well-earned immortal sorrows begin. But we also keep our eyes open to our own lives knowing that temptation and sin are around every corner. We commit to constantly evaluating ourselves so that we can be as dedicated to righteousness as those lost people were to their sin. And we rest and worship in the promise that one day we will experience the renewed kingdom of God and will witness our blessed Redeemer sitting on His glorious throne.

CHAPTER 3

OVERSTAYING YOUR WELCOME

EZEKIEL 8–11

My childhood is not a time of my life that I look back on with fondness. After my parents divorced, certain situations led me to the foster care system. There were several settings in which I was housed for a time, but they were short-lived. Finally, I was placed in a home with a family. However, for me, it was neither home nor family. It was simply a building in which I could receive food and shelter along with a group of people who had love for one another, but none for me.

This situation was tenable for a time. But the older I got, the more my feelings of isolation grew. In my mid-teens, these feelings became so strong that I decided to end my life. That was when, through a miraculous set of circumstances, I was introduced to Yeshua. My life transformed in an instant. For the first time, I experienced true joy. In my elation, I shared about my wonderful conversion with my foster parents, assuring them that they, too, could have the same kind of relationship with the Messiah that I had. They promptly kicked me out.

It was not easy to leave. There had been times of laughter, and eventually, a certain bond had been formed. But as I walked away from the closed door, I knew there was no going back.

There are few places more inhospitable than those where you are known but not wanted. For God, Jerusalem had become that place. In a series of vignettes and prophecies, Ezekiel now described how the children of Israel had quite literally turned their backs to their God, demonstrably showed that He was no longer wanted in His own house, and made it clear that their loyalty belonged to other gods. You didn't need to be omniscient to read the signs. Having no interest in staying where He was not wanted, the glory of God left the temple.

A Tragedy in Four Acts (8)

Before God relocated His glory, He first wanted to make it clear why He was packing up and heading out. Once again, Ezekiel time-stamped the date, placing it on September 17, 592 BC, a little more than 13 months after his first vision and calling. The prophet was having a gathering of some sort in his house with several elders. While they were all sitting around, God stepped in, and He was full of fire. "Then I looked, and there was a likeness, like the appearance of fire—from the appearance of His waist and downward, fire; and from His waist and upward, like the appearance of brightness, like the color of amber" (Ezekiel 8:2).

No one other than Ezekiel was privy to the vision, but I'm sure the rest knew something was going on by the look on the prophet's face. Reaching out what appeared to be His hand, God took a lock of Ezekiel's hair and transported him by the Holy Spirit, in a vision, to the temple in Jerusalem. The glory of God was still in that holy building in all its shining brilliance, the same as in the prophet's first vision. It seems that God would not leave until it was fully understood why He was done inhabiting the place.

Act 1: The Image of Jealousy

The location of Ezekiel's arrival was the north gate of the inner court, one of three gates to that part of the temple grounds. The others were the south and the east. There, in that holy place, stood an idol—what Ezekiel called "an image of jealousy." Whose jealousy? God's. Imagine a woman bringing her boyfriend into the family room, snuggling up to her beau on the couch, flipping on the television, then starting a make-out session. All the while, her husband is watching the disrespectful display from his easy chair. The very act is designed to affront and stoke jealousy. God's words to Ezekiel reflected His hurt and anger.

> Son of man, do you see what they are doing, the great abominations that the house of Israel commits here, to make Me go far away from My sanctuary? Now turn again, you will see greater abominations (verse 6).

According to God's words, the adulterous acts of the house of Israel were intentionally designed to drive Him away. That's understandable on Israel's part. It can get awkward trying to carry on an affair while your husband is sitting in the room.

Note that last line—"you will see greater abominations." That will become the unfortunate repeating chorus that closes each scene of this tragic performance. With every succeeding act, the situation will only get worse.

Act 2: Wicked Wall Art

Indicating a hole in the wall, the Lord next told Ezekiel to dig through. The temple had been built solidly with stone and wood during the time of Solomon. If there were holes that were diggable, that was either God's provision for the vision, or evidence of the temple's disrepair and the disrespect with which the priests treated the holy structure.

Ezekiel dug and found a door. Opening it and stepping in, he saw "every sort of creeping thing, abominable beasts, and all the idols of the house of Israel, portrayed all around on the walls. And there stood before them seventy men of the elders of the house of Israel, and in their midst stood Jaazaniah the son of Shaphan. Each man had a censer in his hand, and a thick cloud of incense went up" (verses 10-11). While the elders in Babylonian exile were seeking wisdom from Ezekiel in his home, the elders still in Israel were offering incense to idolatrous drawings. And this was being done in the temple, of all places!

Why were they doing this? Because they felt betrayed and abandoned by God. "The Lord does not see us, the Lord has forsaken the land," they complained (verse 12). What they didn't realize was that the glory of the Lord was still there, standing at the entrance to the inner court. He wasn't hiding. They just needed to look for Him with pure and repentant hearts. But it was much easier for them to say this was a "you" problem than a "me" problem. "God is doing us wrong; we're not doing Him wrong. Because He has abandoned us, we'll draw our own gods on the walls and worship them."

But if you think that's bad, just wait. Their rebellion will only get worse.

Act 3: Weeping for Tammuz

Tammuz was a young, good-looking Babylonian god who became smitten with the goddess Ishtar. Thus began the age-old story of boy falls in love with girl, boy marries girl, girl murders boy. This deicide broke the hearts of womankind everywhere. So, every fall, the season in which their handsome hero met his end, women from all around the Fertile Crescent would gather in groups to shed tears for this fallen paramour.

To keep the men from rolling their eyes at their wives crying over some sappy love story, the death of Tammuz was also tied to a bigger picture of seasonal changes. When spring came with its bright vibrancy, the people would identify this with the rebirth of the joyful and beautiful Tammuz. Once the leaves changed in autumn and all the green turned brown, it was then acceptable for the women to mourn the end of another season of Tammuzian splendor.

This weeping worship of a dead god was blatantly taking place at the door of the temple's north gate. In what feels like a dismissive and disgusted manner, God said to Ezekiel, "Have you seen this, O son of man? Turn again, you will see greater abominations than these." It's like God gave an eye roll, an "Oy vey," and a "Keep walking. There's worse ahead."

Act #4: Sun Worship

Now we come to the final act in this drama, and this one concludes with a scene worthy of a Shakesperean tragedy.

> So He brought me into the inner court of the LORD's house; and there, at the door of the temple of the LORD, between the porch and the altar, were about twenty-five men with their backs toward the temple of the LORD and their faces toward the east, and they were worshiping the sun toward the east (verse 16).

In that one verse, the entire failure of both Israel and Judah is depicted. When Solomon built this temple, He offered a prayer of dedication in which he pled:

> If Your people Israel are defeated before an enemy because they have sinned against You, and return and confess Your name, and pray and make supplication before You in this temple, then hear from heaven and forgive the sin of Your people Israel, and bring them back to the land which You gave to them and their fathers (2 Chronicles 6:24-25).

The 25 men in the temple were in the very situation about which Solomon had prayed. They were defeated. Their foes had already deported many of the people. Now, the enemy was coming back for more. All these spiritual leaders needed to do was to turn toward the temple, confess and make supplication before God, and the Lord would forgive them and take care of the problem. Instead, their backs were toward the temple and their faces were toward the sun. They ignored the Creator and sought solace and help from a mere creation. Because of this blatant and arrogant rebellion, God told Ezekiel, "Therefore I also will act in fury. My eye will not spare nor will I have pity; and though they cry in My ears with a loud voice, I will not hear them" (Ezekiel 8:18).

I would be remiss moving on without mentioning allusions to the work and person of Yeshua in the false worship of these people of Judah. As I mentioned, every fall, the mythical Tammuz would die and lie in the grave for months. Then spring would come, and Tammuz would resurrect to the joy and celebration of all. This was an annual celebration throughout many nations. When Jesus was crucified, He, too, went into the grave. Three days later, He was resurrected. But when He returned, it was for good. No annual event is needed. One time for all time. "This [Jesus], after He had offered one sacrifice for sins forever, sat down at the right hand of God, from that time waiting till His enemies are made His footstool" (Hebrews 10:12-13).

As for the elders who turned their faces toward the sun, their timing was off. The Lord promised a coming era when all will turn and worship the Sun: "To you who fear My name the Sun of Righteousness shall arise with healing in His wings; and you shall go out and grow fat like stall-fed calves" (Malachi 4:2). Yeshua will come again, and all will face Him and give Him glory and praise. So much hope; so much promise. All of it is to be found in the Lord. Sadly, the Israelites of Ezekiel's day missed it all.

The Mark of the Best (9)

At the end of chapter 8, God promised to act in fury. In chapter 9, we see that fury carried out. A divine call is made for those who have charge over the city.

> Suddenly six men came from the direction of the upper gate, which faces north, each with his battle-ax in his hand. One man among them was clothed with linen and had a writer's inkhorn at his side. They went in and stood beside the bronze altar (Ezekiel 9:2-3).

I must admit that I particularly like the way the New King James words this passage. The ESV and NRSV both describe what these men carry as "weapons of slaughter," while the NIV gives the innocuous title of "deadly weapon." But with the NKJV, I picture gigantic, Viking-looking behemoths stepping forward with horned helmets on their heads and battle-axes in their hands, ready to go berserk throughout the city. Along with them came one more, a scribe-ish looking man wearing linen and carrying a pen and ink.

Together, they gathered by the bronze altar to receive their mission. The man with the pen was told to go through the city and find all those who mourned over the sinful state of Jerusalem and the people of God. Believe it or not, some of them were still out there. It had been only 13 years earlier when faithful Daniel was taken. Then, just four years ago, Ezekiel was hauled away to exile, and his commitment to God was enough for him to be called into the prophet profession. Like that remnant of hair tucked away in the seam of Ezekiel's garment, there will always be some who remain true to the Lord.

As the man found the faithful, he was to give them a mark. In contrast to the mark of the beast in the end times, this would be the mark of the best. In Revelation 14, an angel warned that anyone who received the mark of the beast and worshipped his image would receive the fullness of God's fury. But here in Ezekiel, the mark on one's forehead was a good thing.

> To the [battle-axe guys] He said in my hearing, "Go after him through the city and kill; do not let your eye spare, nor have any pity. Utterly slay old and young men, maidens and little children and women; but do not come near anyone on whom is the mark; and begin at My sanctuary." So they began with the elders who were before the temple. Then He said to them, "Defile the temple, and fill the courts with the slain. Go out!" And they went out and killed in the city (Ezekiel 9:5-7).

What must Ezekiel have witnessed? I think of some of the videos I see as I disseminate news through my Telegram channel. The brutality of this world is sometimes so great that I have to put my phone down and walk away for a time. And that's just watching it on a screen. For Ezekiel, the violence was live and in color. It's no wonder he once again found himself on his face, this time crying out, "Ah, Lord GOD! Will You destroy all the remnant of Israel in pouring out Your fury on Jerusalem?" (verse 8).

When David cried out for God to stay His hand of punishment against Israel as a result of his own sin, we read that He told the angel of the Lord, "It is enough; now restrain your hand" (1 Chronicles 21:15). God's response to Ezekiel's pleading was very different. He said, "My eye will neither spare, nor will I have pity, but I will recompense their deeds on their own head" (Ezekiel 9:10). The people of Israel had simply gone too far. There would be no more respite.

This is the harsh punishment for unrighteousness. Some will receive a taste of its bitterness here on Earth. But for everyone without the salvation that comes through Yeshua, they will experience it after this life is over. And for them, it will not end.

The Glory Departs (10)

Between the people's blatant disrespect and verbal abuse of God and the Lord's clear demonstration of what was in store for those who had abandoned Him, it was evident that the time had finally come for the glory of the Lord to hit the road. As Ezekiel stood there with the linen-clad scribe and the Viking-ish men with their blood-dripping battle-axes, the firmament appeared again with the throne sitting upon it. A voice came from the throne, saying to the scribe, "Go in among the wheels, under the cherub, fill your hands with coals of fire from among the cherubim, and scatter them over the city" (Ezekiel 10:2).

Wait, the wheels are back? Yes, they are. When the firmament had appeared, the creaturely cherubim returned. And, if you remember, a creaturely cherub never went anywhere without his trusty wheel. Ezekiel described the scene as the man in linen obeyed the command.

> Now the cherubim were standing on the south side of the temple when the man went in, and the cloud filled the inner court. Then the glory of the LORD went up from the cherub, and paused over the threshold of the temple; and the house was filled with the cloud, and the court was full of the brightness of the LORD's glory. And the sound of the wings of the cherubim was heard even in the outer court, like the voice of Almighty God when He speaks (verses 3-5).

Earlier, we looked at a brief portion of Solomon's prayer at the temple's dedication. When he finished, something wondrous happened in the sight of all who were watching the ceremony.

> When Solomon had finished praying, fire came down from heaven and consumed the burnt offering and the

sacrifices; and the glory of the LORD filled the temple. And the priests could not enter the house of the LORD, because the glory of the LORD had filled the LORD's house. When all the children of Israel saw how the fire came down, and the glory of the LORD on the temple, they bowed their faces to the ground on the pavement, and worshiped and praised the LORD, saying: "For He is good, for His mercy endures forever" (2 Chronicles 7:1-3).

For all the years since, the Lord's glory had remained. Through the terrible times of Kings Abijah and Jehoram, the illegitimate usurpation by Queen Athaliah, the blood-drenched reign of Manasseh, and the sin-filled incompetence of the final four monarchs, the long-suffering love of the Lord had allowed His glory to continue residence in the temple. But finally, enough was enough. The Lord's patience had been tried beyond its breaking point. The glory of the Lord lifted from the temple and hovered at the structure's threshold.

The man in linen was reminded to get the fire, and he received a handful of flames from one of the cherubim. He then turned and walked out. We don't read what he did with his burning handful. Fire, though, is representative of God's judgment. Because the man was the one who guided the axmen earlier, we can assume that he took the flames and scattered them over Jerusalem as a sign of its impending destruction.

We can't blame Ezekiel for not following linen-man because he was once again taken in by the surrounding sights. What follows in the middle part of chapter 10 is somewhat of a reprise of chapter 1 in Ezekiel's description of the cherubim and their companions. We do get one new insight—a name for the wheels. "As for the wheels, they were called in my hearing, 'Wheel'" (Ezekiel 10:13). This is a very matter-of-fact and descriptive name, much like naming your dog "Dog."

It was finally time for the glory to go.

> Then the glory of the LORD departed from the threshold of the temple and stood over the cherubim. And the cherubim lifted their wings and mounted up from the earth in my sight. When they went out, the wheels were beside them; and they stood at the door of the east gate of the LORD's house, and the glory of the God of Israel was above them (verses 18-19).

The glory of the Lord rose up over the temple grounds, but God seemed reluctant to leave. Hovering over the cherubim, He made it as far as the East Gate and then paused. You can sense the longing the Almighty had for the repentance and restoration of His people. This reminds me of a husband saying his last goodbye to his wife before the casket is closed. You know you have to let go, but that final parting is painful beyond words.

A Tale of Two Prophecies (11)

There was one more scene for Ezekiel to witness before the vision was over, and this time, he would be a participant. The glory of the Lord, along with the cherubim, had paused over the Eastern Gate. Now that the prophet had a clear view of the area, he saw a gathering of 25 leaders who were discussing the message they should communicate to the people. This reminds me of a consortium of media execs gathering to determine what spin they would give to a news story. The Spirit pointed them out to the prophet and said:

> Son of man, these are the men who devise iniquity and give wicked counsel in this city, who say, "The time is not near to build houses; this city is the caldron, and we are the meat." Therefore prophesy against them, prophesy, O son of man! (Ezekiel 11:2-4).

While on the surface the message of these men appears to be negative, it wasn't. An alternative reading of the first line of their spin is, "Is this not the time to build houses?" That phrasing gives the gist of their words. According to them, the people are safe in the city. The walls of Jerusalem are like the solid metal of a caldron. Inside, they are safe like the meat that is cooking for the evening meal.

It was their self-sufficient, "We've got this on our own, so who needs God?" attitude that was so grating to the Lord. Not only did these men believe this lie, but they were in a position to deceive the rest of the city into believing they were perfectly fine to just keep doing what they were doing. These men were liars of the most heinous kind. Not only would they take themselves down, they would ensure the deaths of thousands more. God, in His message to these men, declared:

> "Your slain whom you have laid in its midst, they are the meat, and this city is the caldron; but I shall bring you out of the midst of it. You have feared the sword; and I will bring a sword upon you," says the Lord God. "And I will bring you out of its midst, and deliver you into the hands of strangers, and execute judgments on you. You shall fall by the sword. I will judge you at the border of Israel. Then you shall know that I am the Lord" (verses 7-10).

There was nothing good in store for those remaining in Jerusalem. To emphasize this point, as Ezekiel was still prophesying, one of the elders, Pelatiah the son of Benaiah, fell to the ground dead. Imagine the fear and shock that must have ripped through the hearts of the other 24 men. Even Ezekiel fell to the ground and cried out, "Ah, Lord God! Will You make a complete end of the remnant of Israel?" (verse 13).

These elders deserved the fate that was awaiting them. They were the exact opposite of watchmen. When a watchman saw a threat, he was to cry at the top of his lungs, "Danger!" But as the hordes of Babylon laid siege against the city of Jerusalem, these men instead put on their best used-chariot salesmen smiles and ensured, "Safety, my friends. Safety." Pelatiah, son of Benaiah, was a demonstration of what was awaiting those who so blatantly disregarded their duty. So much death. So much destruction. But we can't let these harsh times cause us to forget that Israel is, has been, and always will be God's chosen people. While firm discipline is necessary to return an out-of-control nation to sanity, it is only for a reason and for a season. A day is coming when there will be a joyous reunion between the Lord and His people. Following Ezekiel's days, the reunion was grand but imperfect. In the far view, it will be wondrous and complete. God communicated this intention through a three-part promise.

First, He said He would take care of His people while they were in exile. He promised, "Although I have cast them far off among the Gentiles, and although I have scattered them among the countries, yet I shall be a little sanctuary for them in the countries where they have gone" (verse 16). Yes, the exiles were far from Jerusalem's city walls, but God would still protect them. Besides, city walls can be brought down, as would soon be proven by Babylon. But nobody can break through God's barrier.

The phrase "little sanctuary" in verse 16 is a translation of the Hebrew phrase מִקְדָּשׁ מְעַט (*mikdash me'at*). The word *mikdash* means "temple," so a *mikdash me'at* is a "little temple." God told the Israelites that no matter where His people went, He would dwell in the holy places they created for Him. It is from this specific prophecy that the entire concept of synagogues arose. *Synagogue* is the Greek translation of the Hebrew *bet knesset*, both of which mean "house of gathering" or "place of gathering."

The Jews of the diaspora gathered in their little temples with the assurance from Ezekiel 11:16 that God would be there with them. But they did so recognizing that their synagogues were only small versions of the real temple. In fact, many synagogues in America and in the West are called temples, acknowledging the fact that they are most holy sites. While the little temples suffice for now, there is the expectation that one day all Jews will gather in the real temple rebuilt in its rightful place in Jerusalem. That hope is found in the next verse.

When the time of the exile is complete, according to the second part of the promise, the Lord would bring His people back home. "Therefore say, 'Thus says the Lord God: "I will gather you from the peoples, assemble you from the countries where you have been scattered, and I will give you the land of Israel"'" (verse 17). This punishment is for a purpose, and eventually its goal will be achieved. At that time there will be a homecoming of the exiles, which we can read about in the narratives of Ezra and Nehemiah.

The third and final element of this promise jumps ahead to a future time when God will gather His chosen people to prepare them for Yeshua's millennial reign.

> Then I will give them one heart, and I will put a new spirit within them, and take the stony heart out of their flesh, and give them a heart of flesh, that they may walk in My statutes and keep My judgments and do them; and they shall be My people, and I will be their God (verses 19-20).

What a wonderful promise! The day is coming when the entire Jewish people will be right with God, loving Him and serving Him as was intended from the day the promise was given to Abraham. "But, Amir, why are you saying this is in the future? Isn't this exactly what God did when He brought the exiles back to Jerusalem?" Unfortunately, no. Otherwise, there would not have been a need for a Zechariah to tell the returnees to get their acts together and a Haggai to push them to get off their backsides and get the temple built. And when you read Nehemiah and especially Ezra, it's very clear that these are a people who are much better than they used to be. However, they are far from being what they will one day become.

Ezekiel himself points to the distant future nature of this promise later in chapter 36 of his book. As we'll see in more detail when we get there, one more regathering of God's people will take place in the land of Israel. It is then that this spiritual transformation will take place, and God will be able to say that both in name and in relationship, "they shall be My people, and I will be their God" (verse 20).

With these final prophecies stated, it was time for the glory of God to let the hand of His people slip from His own so that He could turn His back and leave. "And the glory of the Lord went up from the midst of the city and stood on the mountain, which is on the east side of the city" (verse 23). One last look from the Mount of Olives, and the glory was gone.

The vision ended. Ezekiel found himself back with the other exiles, and he told them of the long, strange adventure he had experienced.

It's a tragic story, but let me add a happy coda to this sad symphony of separation. When the glory of the Lord lifted from the ark of the covenant set between the cherubim, it rose above the temple, then traveled to the East Gate. After pausing, the glory moved to the Mount of Olives, from which it then rose to heaven. For some of you, that location may already have your prophecy sensors pinging.

God wasn't done with the people of Israel. He still had a plan for them. He had taken His glory from them, but He would bring it back—twice. A little more than 600 years later, a man sat on a donkey as the animal cantered down that same Mount of Olives. The rider who was astride the animal was more than just a man; He was the God-man—Jesus the Messiah. In His human body resided the full glory of the Lord. As Jesus rode toward Jerusalem, the people called out to Him, "Hosanna to the Son of David! 'Blessed is He who comes in the name of the Lord!' Hosanna in the highest!"

(Matthew 21:9). As they directed their praises to heaven, they didn't realize that the recipient of their worship was right in front of them.

When the Lord reached Jerusalem, He went straight to the temple. Once there, He angrily turned over the tables of those who were profiting off the worship of God, crying out, "It is written, 'My house shall be called a house of prayer,' but you have made it a 'den of thieves'" (verse 13). The glory of the Lord had returned to the temple and sadly found it still in a state of spiritual disarray. Rather than it being awash with idolatry and adultery, it was drowning in profiteering and religiosity. His time at the place dedicated to His name was short. Soon He was back on the Mount of Olives, from which He once again left, taking His glory with Him (Acts 1:6-12).

That first return was not intended to be a permanent residency; it was merely a visitation. A day is coming when He will be back to stay. When the glory of the Lord returns once again in the person of the resurrected Christ, to where will it come? The same location that it left, then came back to, then left once again—the Mount of Olives.

> In that day His feet will stand on the Mount of Olives, which faces Jerusalem on the east. And the Mount of Olives shall be split in two, from east to west, making a very large valley; half of the mountain shall move toward the north and half of it toward the south (Zechariah 14:4).

It is at that final return that Jerusalem will become the home of the eternal King, and the glory of the Lord will reside in the holy city forever!

CHAPTER 4

TOP-DOWN SIN

EZEKIEL 12-14

Each day I am deep into the news. My Telegram channel is a ravenous beast that constantly needs to be fed more. It is essential for people to have the most up-to-date and relevant information available, and I relish the opportunities that are often provided when I can filter geopolitical stories through a biblical lens. As I mentioned in the last chapter, as I am surrounded by the world's ugliness, it can sometimes be difficult not to become jaded and even pessimistic. How do people do these things to one another? Where does that level of hatred come from?

I particularly found myself struggling with this inner anger and melancholy following the massacre of October 7, 2023. Like anyone in Israel, I grew up recognizing the absolute loathing of Palestinians for my people. You learn to live with it, and you make sure you don't put yourself into any situations in which you are alone and outnumbered. But what took place that day was beyond the actions of hatred. It was pure evil. In the days and months following the attack, I often found myself, during my numerous sleepless nights listening for terrorist footsteps outside my house, wondering how anyone can commit such acts. It wouldn't take me long to come to an obvious conclusion. Sin is generational. It is passed from great-grandfather to grandfather to father to son.

At home, in school, in mosques, Palestinians are taught that the most honoring sacrifice they can offer to Allah is to martyr themselves while killing Jews. We know this from the educational materials we've found in their schools and homes, and from the testimonies of many who have escaped that culture of death. But this kind of hatred is not only found in Hamas households in Gaza, Syria, and Judea and Samaria. It resides all over the world between nations, between tribes, and between people groups.

Acts of sin carried out by one generation after another are not only found in racial animosity. Deceptive beliefs passed down from parent to child are also at the heart of most faulty religious traditions. When you think of a young girl being brought up in the Buddhist nation of Bhutan or a boy being reared in an atheistic home in Western Europe, it's difficult not to step back and think, *They don't stand a chance for salvation. Maybe there is a little more possibility with the European boy because there are at least some vestiges of God still around the continent. But the Bhutanese girl? How can the gospel even reach her?*

This ignorance of righteousness is the situation in which many during the siege and fall of Jerusalem found themselves. Yes, they were from a country that technically belonged to God. But most people had jettisoned Him from their pantheon generations ago, replacing Him with high places, household gods, Asherah poles, and the fire god, Molech. Idolatry was what the people knew. Yes, the population of Israel were considered God-lovers because they lived in the Promised Land, but only in the same way as the people of the Netherlands or of Finland are Christian because they live in Christian Europe.

Generation after generation of Israelites had sought after other gods. What made matters worse was that their leaders, both political and religious, were the ones heading the charge. The kings were wicked, the priests were compromised, and most of the so-called prophets were making their living by telling the citizens only what they wanted to hear. Tickling the people's ears will get you rewarded, and you may even receive a commissioning by the king. Prophesying doom and gloom, however, will get you ostracized and you'll probably starve. Like everything else in this world, just follow the money.

The generations of unrighteousness had not gone unnoticed in the heavenly realms. God had seen the way that year after year the people had drifted further away from Him. He'd had enough. Now He was ready to call them out for their rejection and bad leadership. As we read through the next three chapters of Ezekiel, we'll see Him challenging the king, the prophets, the elders, and, finally, the people.

Catching of a King (12)

God came to speak to Ezekiel once again, but this time, it wasn't with a grandiose display or a visionary journey to Jerusalem. It was simply a new instance of the Creator tasking one of His creations to be His mouthpiece to the exiles. Starting off, the Lord reminded Ezekiel of whom he was dealing with, saying, "Son of man, you dwell in the midst of a rebellious house, which has eyes to see but does not see, and ears to hear but does not hear; for they are a rebellious house" (Ezekiel 12:2). In other words, a brief reiteration of the current futility of the prophet's mission.

Following that morale boost, God gave Ezekiel his new mission. He was to gather up his belongings as he had done when he was first taken into captivity. People watching him would know exactly what he was doing, because they had all been forced to do the same thing years earlier. Once packed, he was to haul his possessions out into the open. Then, when the timing was right, he was to dig through a wall and act like he was making his escape.

Dig through the wall in their sight, and carry your belongings out through it. In their sight you shall bear them on your shoulders and carry them out at twilight; you shall cover your face, so that you cannot see the ground, for I have made you a sign to the house of Israel (verses 5-6).

Digging a hole through the wall and making an escape from the Babylonian invaders—this was certainly a demonstration of a near-future event for the exiles. But for those of you who may be a little more familiar with the historical happenings surrounding the fall of Jerusalem, this description may have set your Spidey-senses tingling. After Ezekiel went through with this practical demonstration, the Lord spoke again and made His point even clearer.

Say to them, "Thus says the Lord GOD: 'This burden concerns the prince in Jerusalem and all the house of Israel who are among them.'" Say, "I am a sign to you. As I have done, so shall it be done to them; they shall be carried away into captivity." And the prince who is among them shall bear his belongings on his shoulder at twilight and go out. They shall dig through the wall to carry them out through it. He shall cover his face, so that he cannot see the ground with his eyes. I will also spread My net over him, and he shall be caught in My snare. I will bring him to Babylon, to the land of the Chaldeans; yet he shall not see it, though he shall die there (verses 10-13).

God was prophesying against King Zedekiah, the prince in Jerusalem. He said that, like Ezekiel, the monarch himself would pack up his belongings. He would then sneak past the wall, and attempt an escape. But he wouldn't get away. He would be captured and brought to Babylon, where the king would die. An interesting addition was that, despite the king being transported to Nebuchadnezzar's capital, he wouldn't lay eyes on it. The question of what that strange twist meant must have swirled amongst the exiles until the time five or six years later when the prophecy was fulfilled.

In time, Nebuchadnezzar and his army breached the wall of Jerusalem. King Zedekiah and what was left of his army escaped through a side gate and fled the city.

> But the army of the Chaldeans [Babylonians] pursued the king, and they overtook Zedekiah in the plains of Jericho. All his army was scattered from him. So they took the king and brought him up to the king of Babylon at Riblah in the land of Hamath, and he pronounced judgment on him. Then the king of Babylon killed the sons of Zedekiah before his eyes. And he killed all the princes of Judah in Riblah. He also put out the eyes of Zedekiah; and the king of Babylon bound him in bronze fetters, took him to Babylon, and put him in prison till the day of his death (Jeremiah 52:8-12).

The prophecy was fulfilled exactly as it was told. A blinded king was taken in chains to Babylon, where he died a prisoner. Imagine being one of the exiles and hearing the story of the fall of Jerusalem. When the teller of the tale came to the point where Zedekiah's eyes were put out, a gasp must have sounded from the listeners. The "not seeing it" mystery had been solved, but in such a tragic way. It is no wonder that God finished this prophecy, saying once again, "Then they shall know that I am the LORD" (Ezekiel 12:16). A promise given, a promise fulfilled.

No Empty Promises (12)

It's interesting to see this quick turnaround of prophecy and fulfillment, particularly when we continue reading this chapter. Today, there are many who mock me and others who believe in a pretribulation rapture, saying, "Amir, according to you, the Bible says that the rapture is imminent. Since that was two thousand years ago, then either God must have gotten delayed, or *imminent* doesn't really mean 'imminent.'" If I could have included a smug-looking emoji with that sentence, I would have.

First, I am not the keeper of God's timeline. If you feel that He has "delayed" anything, feel free to take that up with Him. As for *imminent*, that word fits the rapture perfectly, and I would say that any struggle you have with it has nothing to do with God's timeline but with your definition. Our dear friends Mr. Merriam and Mr. Webster defined *imminent* as "ready to take place: happening soon."[3] The first of the two similar definitions is spot on for the rapture. There is nothing, nor has there been anything, that has kept that airborne union from taking place other than the longsuffering mercy of God. All the ducks are in a row, and everyone is just waiting on word from the Boss.

It is in the context of God's longsuffering mercy that we find the answer to the second part of Merriam and Webster's definition, "happening soon." In the early church, there were the same kind of endtimes naysayers that we find in today's hallowed halls. Challenging the prophecies of the teachers, they said, "Where is the promise of His coming? For since the fathers fell asleep, all things continue as they were from the beginning of creation" (2 Peter 3:4). The apostle Peter was quick to address their impatience, reminding them that God doesn't see time the way they do and that when they feel like He's delaying, He's doing it for a reason.

> Beloved, do not forget this one thing, that with the Lord one day is as a thousand years, and a thousand years as one day. The Lord is not slack concerning His promise, as some count slackness, but is longsuffering toward us, not

willing that any should perish but that all should come to repentance (verses 8-9).

Peter's statement was both an encouragement and a harsh rebuke. Along with his affirmation that the time of Christ's return will come, he challenged the cynics to quit selfishly thinking only of themselves. Of course, we are all ready to go to heaven and see our Savior face to face. But there are other people whom God still wants to bring into His kingdom. So, suck it up, buttercup. Your time will come when the time comes. Quit trying to steal another person's opportunity at salvation just because you're impatient.

In the same way that there are people today saying, "Where is God?," there were those in Jerusalem asking that question. In response, the Lord quoted a common Jerusalem proverb, which stated, "The days are prolonged, and every vision fails" (Ezekiel 12:22). The people were saying this to criticize what they believed were the false prophecies being proclaimed by those who were, in reality, the true prophets. In essence, they were complaining, "They're telling us that the end is near, but I'm still alive. So keep up with your blah blah blah, Jeremiah. We're done listening."

God was utterly fed up with these shortsighted liars. To Ezekiel, He said, "Son of man, look, the house of Israel is saying, 'The vision that he sees is for many days from now, and he prophesies of times far off.' Therefore say to them, 'Thus says the Lord GOD: "None of My words will be postponed any more, but the word which I speak will be done,"' says the Lord GOD'" (verses 27-28).

No more delays. There are no empty promises. Judgment is coming, and it's coming now.

Man-Made Prophecies (13)

Despite the idolatry and wickedness of the people of Israel, the Mosaic religious leaders of Ezekiel's time still held a great amount of authority. When the people were in a bind and felt they needed to hear a word from God, the priests alone were the ones who could read from the Torah, the Histories, the Wisdom, and the Prophets. If a more contemporaneous message was needed, they could even turn to the popular prophets, who could give them a direct message from the Almighty.

Allegedly.

For every Jeremiah and Ezekiel speaking the true words of God, there were a wagonful of Hananiahs and Shemaiahs who attained their honored positions by conjuring up words the people wanted to hear and putting them in the mouth of the Lord. Why would they lie this way? Everyone has got to make a living, and along with the financial tribute that folks would give to a "good-news speaking" prophet, there was power and prestige to be had. In other words, false prophecy was a pretty good gig if you could get it.

Before we condemn the people for following these forth-tellers of God's supposed rose-colored words, we need to take a look at the church today. How many of the nation's largest congregations are centered on the prosperity gospel and Kingdom Now theology? People want to hear from God. But if they are given a choice between hearing God's good news or His bad news, most people—particularly those who tend toward the shallow end of the faith—will say, "Tickle my ears with something good, because this world is bringing me down."

Now picture yourself in Jerusalem. The siege walls are up. The food is running out. Twice already the city has been overrun and people deported. You find two prophets standing before you. One is saying, "Yeah, you guys deserve this. It's going to get really ugly, then you're all going to die." The other is saying, "Don't worry, friends. It'll get better. God is going to save us." Which one would you want to listen to? The promise of hope is a powerful lure, even if it is a lie.

The current situation for Ezekiel was slightly different than it had been for the prophets of the past. His audience was not the people in the city, but their exiled loved ones who still held out hope for those left behind and for Jerusalem itself. Even in Babylon, Israelite prophets were falsely claiming peace, telling everyone that their families would be okay. The people flocked to these liars, soaking in their deceptions to quell their sorrow.

All the while, God was watching. He heard the words of the deceptive prophets in Jerusalem and amongst the exiles, and He was done with them. Calling Ezekiel forward, He said, "Son of man, prophesy against the prophets of Israel who prophesy, and say to those who prophesy out of their own heart, 'Hear the word of the LORD!'" (Ezekiel 13:2). No longer would He allow others to put words into His mouth. He was about to call them out for the liars that they were.

> "Because you have spoken nonsense and envisioned lies, therefore I am indeed against you," says the Lord GOD. "My hand will be against the prophets who envision futility and who divine lies; they shall not be in the assembly of My people, nor be written in the record of the house of Israel, nor shall they enter into the land of Israel. Then you shall know that I am the Lord GOD" (verses 8-9).

Because of their false predictions, the prophets had created a god that didn't exist. The Lord, the true God, told the people that He was going to bring these fake spokesmen and the city down. When that destruction occurred, it would become crystal clear to those in Jerusalem and to the exiles in Babylon who was the true Lord God.

To emphasize the pitiful weakness of the false prophets' words, God presented an illustration. The defenses of Jerusalem were like a wall that the people had built up against the Babylonians. To strengthen the wall, the prophets had added a coating of plaster made up of their words of hope and strength. But the plaster was weak. They hadn't allowed it to sit and temper before applying it. Thus, when God would allow the Babylonians to blow in like a storm, the wall would collapse. With power, the enemy would sweep through the city, consuming the prophets and those who followed them.

> Thus will I accomplish My wrath on the wall and on those who have plastered it with untempered mortar; and I will say to you, "The wall is no more, nor those who plastered it, that is, the prophets of Israel who prophesy concerning Jerusalem, and who see visions of peace for her when there is no peace," says the Lord God (verses 15-16).

People were searching for hope anywhere they could find it, whether it was through false teachings, idols, or blasphemous sacrifices. Prophetesses in Jerusalem were even sewing magical talismans to their clothing in the hopes of warding off the coming evil. Not surprisingly, they were also doing a good business selling these safety charms to a panicked people, hunting them down with their handcrafted lies like one does a bird. God called out these deceivers-for-profit too, saying:

> Behold, I am against your magic charms by which you hunt souls there like birds. I will tear them from your arms, and let the souls go, the souls you hunt like birds. I will also tear off your veils and deliver My people out of your hand, and they shall no longer be as prey in your hand. Then you shall know that I am the Lord (verses 20-21).

These charms were simply one more lie drawing people away from the truth. People believed the charms had the power to protect them, when instead they should have been relying on the All-Powerful for their protection. When their magic is ultimately proven false, that's when the deceived will finally recognize the One who always remains true. By that time, though, it will be too late.

Man's Righteousness Versus God's Plan (14)

When James was wrapping up his epistle, he talked about praying for the sick and anointing them with oil. He continued by writing, "Confess your trespasses to one another, and pray for one another, that you may be healed. The effective, fervent prayer of a righteous man avails much" (James 5:16). The power of prayer is a mysterious concept, and God has purposely kept it ambiguous. If we had this spiritual enigma all figured out, we would probably devise a way to exploit it or twist it into something it was never intended to be. Instead, the scriptural summary on prayer is something like, "Pray at all times. God may answer as you want, or He may not. But He will always answer according to what is best. Unwavering prayers by righteous people have the most effect, but we're not quite sure what having the most effect means. So, just keep on praying."

To demonstrate how far gone the children of God were, God presented two vignettes—the first in exile, and the second in Jerusalem. A group of elders came to visit Ezekiel. They wanted to know from God what they could expect for their future years in Babylon. Because they were among the elite class of exiles, they anticipated a prompt and thorough answer. God's response, however, was, "Yeah, I don't think so."

> Son of man, these men have set up their idols in their hearts, and put before them that which causes them to stumble into iniquity. Should I let Myself be inquired of at all by them? Therefore speak to them, and say to them, "Thus says the Lord GOD: 'Everyone of the house of Israel who sets up his idols in his heart, and puts before him what causes him to stumble into iniquity, and then comes to the prophet, I the LORD will answer him who comes, according to the multitude of his idols, that I may seize the house of Israel by their heart, because they are all estranged from Me by their idols'" (Ezekiel 14:3-5).

We read in James about the power of a righteous man's prayer. But the prayer of an unrighteous person? It falls on deaf ears. How many times have you heard unbelievers complain, "I prayed for healing, but God didn't answer"? Or, "I prayed that God would keep my marriage together, but we still ended up divorced"? When I hear those kinds of statements, I want to shake the person and say, "Why would God answer? What are you basing your request on? God is not your butler. He's not your genie."

In their utter arrogance, these elders came to Ezekiel expecting that God would respond because of their position in the community. But God was not impressed. Somehow, their grandiose title of "elder" didn't intimidate Him. He told Ezekiel to let them know, "They get themselves right with Me, then we'll talk. Until then, I've got better stuff to do."

Ezekiel's focus then switched to the people back in Jerusalem. To the prophet, the Lord announced four judgments on the land upon which the rebellious rabble were living. The first plague was famine. "Son of man, when a land sins against Me by persistent unfaithfulness, I will stretch out My hand against it; I will cut off its supply of bread, send famine on it, and cut off man and beast from it" (verse 13). But before the Lord moved on to the second judgment, He provided an interesting addition. He said that even if Noah, Daniel, and Job were in the land, their righteousness would deliver only themselves (verse 14). We'll deal with those three in a moment.

What follows are more judgments, all presented as hypothetical statements. God said, "If I cause wild beasts to pass through the land, and they empty it, and make it so desolate that no man may pass through because of the beasts…" (verse 15). "If I bring a sword on that land, and say, 'Sword, go through the land,' and I cut off man and beast from it…" (verse 17). And, "If I send a pestilence into that land and pour out My fury on it in blood, and cut off from it man and beast…" (verse 19). So, in total, we have a quartet of famine, wild beasts, the sword, and pestilence ravaging the land. But in each case, the trio of Noah, Daniel, and Job are set up as exemptions to the judgments.

This is an interesting trifecta. All three suffered loss and received great gain. Job lost all he had, but later received back twice as much. Daniel lost his home in Jerusalem and he physically lost any hopes of having a family of his own, but he received back incredible power and influence in two empires. Noah experienced the loss of the global population, but later became the new father of all humanity. The righteousness of all three was known to everyone and celebrated. We have written evidence of each of these three praising God and trusting Him completely. There is no doubt that Noah, Daniel, and Job stand out amongst the most righteous and faithful of all time.

Yet even the prayers of these three righteousness heroes would not be enough to stay the hand of God against Jerusalem. Their prayers would be sufficient for saving their own skins. However, the fate of the great city was already determined. Its sin had condemned it to destruction.

This is the way God works, and it is one more reason we can have such hope about the coming rapture. The fate of the world has already been determined through the words of the prophets and the sinfulness of mankind. The tribulation is coming, a horrific time that will make the fall of Jerusalem pale in comparison. But just as God would not let His righteous trio suffer the fate of the Babylonian destruction, He will not let His righteous church suffer the fate of the tribulation.

"Um, Amir, have you seen the church lately? I don't know that we're quite reaching the Noah-Daniel-Job level with our righteousness." Yes, I have seen the church, and you are exactly right about our overall struggles. But the church doesn't have to reach the level of those men. When God looks at believers, He doesn't see the imperfect righteousness of our own stumbling walks. He sees the perfection of the One who imputed His own sinless righteousness upon us. As Paul wrote, "He made Him who knew no sin to be sin for us, that we might become the righteousness of God in Him" (2 Corinthians 5:21). If the human righteousness of those three men would be enough to save them from the destruction of Jerusalem, then we can rest assured that the unsoiled righteousness of our Savior, Jesus Christ, will be plenty to save His church from the coming wrath.

CHAPTER 5

FAILURE THEATER

EZEKIEL 15–19

A woman sits in an armchair with her right hand gently resting on her left wrist. Straight, light brown hair frames her face, then transitions into soft curls as it cascades past her shoulders. Although her dress is elegant, there is no pretense to her look. No makeup, no jewelry, no piercings. The only adornment to her unextraordinary face is a very subtle, yet intriguingly bemused, smile. And it is that almost imperceptible curvature to the corners of her mouth that has transformed her into one of the most well-known women in history.

In a little more than 90 words, I have attempted to describe to you the subject of a painting. But words can only do so much, and the introduction to this chapter can only be so long. I don't have the space to wax poetic on her high forehead and the off-center part to her hair. There is so much to say about her full cheeks, her straight Italian nose, and her small apple-shaped chin, but I don't have room to elaborate on these details. Alas, I have created a literary situation in which the form of my writing is limited by its function. So instead, I will simply tell you to pick up your phone, open your browser, and type "Mona Lisa." In a fraction of a second, your eyes will communicate to you so much more than my words ever could.

In the next five chapters, the Lord is going to prove the old saying, "A picture is worth a thousand words." He has laid out for us the extent of Israel's sin. He has described their unrighteous activities and justified punishment. But there are still those who look at the violence of Jerusalem's fall and say, "Isn't this a little overboard for a loving God?" They continue to not understand just how heartbreaking and gut-wrenching the nation's adultery was to the Lord. For these people, God is now going to stories and pictures to illustrate their sin, His pain, and the coming judgment.

Israel's Great Blessings

Before we launch into Israel's unrighteousness, it would be good to take just a moment to remind ourselves of the amazing blessings that God gave to Israel. Never was a nation so perfectly set for success. It was like running the 100-meter dash but getting a 50-meter head start. The apostle Paul enumerated the special gifts given to Israel when he wrote:

> I could wish that I myself were accursed from Christ for my brethren, my countrymen according to the flesh, who are Israelites, to whom pertain the adoption, the glory, the covenants, the giving of the law, the service of God, and the promises; of whom are the fathers and from whom, according to the flesh, Christ came, who is over all, the eternally blessed God. Amen (Romans 9:3-5).

In those three verses, a sevenfold blessing for Israel is itemized. First, to Israel was given adoption into God's family. Under the Lord's fathership, being adopted is as good as being naturally born, as it should be. During God's call of Moses as a prophet, He commanded,

"You shall say to Pharaoh, 'Thus says the LORD: "Israel is My son, My firstborn. So I say to you, let My son go that he may serve Me. But if you refuse to let him go, indeed I will kill your son, your firstborn"'" (Exodus 4:22-23).

"But, Amir, this says that Israel is God's firstborn, not that it's His adopted son." In this context, it is the same thing. Even Abraham was already an old man when God called him into His family as His child and as the patriarch of the nation. Besides, Israel can't be the physical firstborn of the Father. That role is already taken by Jesus. Paul was saying that Israel was the first of the adopted children of God.

A second blessing is the glory of the Lord. We've already met this wonderful display of God's Shekinah, or "dwelling" glory, in all its beauty and wonder in two locations. One was in the throne room of the Lord. The second was in the temple in Jerusalem. Sadly, the latter meeting was only a passing encounter. Too soon after, the Lord took His glory from the temple because the sin of Israel had become so great.

Third, God graced Israel with four covenants, as we've already seen. Three of these were the unconditional promises of God found in the Abrahamic, Davidic, and the new covenants. The fourth was contractual in nature and was given through Moses. In the Mosaic covenant, consideration was offered by both parties and a deal was struck. God said, in essence, "You obey, and you will be blessed. But if you disobey, you will be cursed" (see Deuteronomy 30:15-20). The people said, "You betcha." The first generation after the death of Moses chose the former option; the generations following lived out the latter.

Blessing number four is the giving of the law. No other nation was blessed with such wise directives for living properly before the God of heaven. As Moses preached to the people of Israel,

> Therefore be careful to observe [the law]; for this is your wisdom and your understanding in the sight of the peoples who will hear all these statutes, and say, "Surely this great

nation is a wise and understanding people." For what great nation is there that has God so near to it, as the LORD our God is to us, for whatever reason we may call upon Him? And what great nation is there that has such statutes and righteous judgments as are in all this law which I set before you this day? (Deuteronomy 4:6-8).

Israel learned how to live righteously from the One who is perfectly righteous, and how to enjoy holy living from the God who gives definition to the word *holy*.

The service of God is the fifth blessing. The context of Paul's statement in Romans 9:3-5 is temple worship, and it was through the Levitical rules and regulations that the Israelites were provided with the proper way for a sinful people to approach a holy God. Even today, the essence of those rules applies in the reverence we should show to the Lord and the necessity of confession, thanksgiving, intercession, and worship. We would not understand any of that without the template God gave to the people of Israel.

The sixth blessing celebrates the promises given through God. It is because of the Lord's communication to His Israelite children that we understand His plan for this world. In our current context, the prophecies given to Ezekiel provide us with vital information regarding Israel's return to the land and the renewal of the nation in chapters 34, 36, and 37. And it is in chapters 38–39 that we learn of the coming war during which God will stand with His people, supernaturally destroying the enemy. That defense of the nation will come despite Israel not yet standing with Him. How's that for long-suffering love? And it is in Ezekiel 40–48 that we receive an affirmation of the promised coming kingdom, when Christ will rule on the earth. Without God's message to Israel, our future would be a blank page.

The final blessing promised by Paul is the Messiah. When I used to lead tours, there were a number of times when people asked me whether Jesus was a Catholic or a Protestant. Their faces fell when I broke the news to them that Jesus was a Jew. He was born a Jew and was raised a Jew. He followed the Mosaic law and celebrated all the feasts. When He died, He was a Jew. And, yes, when He rose again, He was still a Jew!

It is through this Jewish Messiah that we can find eternal hope. His sacrifice of Himself on the cross is what opened the door for us to receive the free gift of eternal life. All of our hope for eternity rests in what one Jewish man did for us.

So many blessings for one people. With this understanding of the people's great potential, let's now look at their tragic failures. But let's do so remembering that no matter how bad the stories we're about to read may get, God's love for His people never ended. He always keeps His promises, which means He always keeps a remnant.

Good Only to Burn (15)

In the first picture given to Ezekiel, I couldn't help but think of the prophet in his role as watchman. God told Ezekiel back in chapter 3, "If people are sinning and I tell you to warn them, then you need to warn them." In other words, "You've got one job. Don't mess up."

Twelve chapters later, the Lord came to the prophet and asked him about the wood of the grapevine:

> Son of man, how is the wood of the vine better than any other wood, the vine branch which is among the trees of the forest? Is wood taken from it to make any object? Or can men make a peg from it to hang any vessel on? (Ezekiel 15:2-3).

The wood of the vine has one job. It is to conduct water to the branches so that grapes can grow. If it's not carrying out its singular task, then it is utterly useless. The wood is too thin, rickety, and brittle to build furniture out of. Are you looking to build a vine-wood desk or an armoire to keep your clothes in? Good luck connecting all the jutty, angly branches to make a smooth surface. And should you somehow find a way of joining the branches, the moment you put any real weight on it, the wood will shatter to pieces. Once a vine stops feeding its grapes, it has only one use left—toss it into a fire so you can warm your hands.

Israel was created and gifted to produce the most amazing grapes ever grown. But the watchmen had shirked their duty. They were too busy gratifying their own desires to take their shifts on the wall. God told Ezekiel that there were consequences for failed watchmen, and the people of Jerusalem were about to pay the price.

> Thus says the Lord God: "Like the wood of the vine among the trees of the forest, which I have given to the fire for fuel, so I will give up the inhabitants of Jerusalem; and I will set My face against them. They will go out from one fire, but another fire shall devour them. Then you shall know that I am the Lord, when I set My face against them" (verses 6-7).

An Unbreakable Love (16)

Once again, like a Shakespearean tragedy, chapter 16 of Ezekiel's book is difficult to read. It's a heartrending tale of God's love and care for the helpless nation of Israel. Upon discovering the hopeless, vulnerable orphan, God gave her life and hope, beauty, and riches. He provided her with food and comfort and gave her an identity above all others—the wife of the Almighty. What people would not be grateful beyond measure for the amazing provision of the Lord God?

The children of Israel, that's who. Not only was this bride ungrateful for all that the Lord had lavished upon her, but she passed on all His great blessings to her adulterous lovers.

We all know stories of adultery. Some of you, undoubtedly, have experienced it in a marriage. The heartbreak is tremendous. Trust is shattered, often irreparably. But what Israel did to God was beyond the extramarital pale. It's not necessary to get into the details, because we all know how depraved their actions were. Suffice it to say, in this chapter alone, Ezekiel used the word "harlot" twelve times, "harlotry" ten times, and variations of the word "abomination" ten times.

There is often a tendency for people to compare the blackness of others' sins with the only slightly grayish nature of their own. They're like the Pharisee in Jesus' parable of the two men praying in the temple. As the holy man raised his voice in self-aggrandizing supplication, he side-eyed another petitioner who was making a scene as he grievously repented. Shaking his head, the Pharisee prayed, "God, I thank You that I am not like other men—extortioners, unjust, adulterers, or even as this tax collector" (Luke 18:11).

That was the arrogant attitude of the southern kingdom of Judah. It had been nearly 130 years since the Assyrians had poured into the northern kingdom of Samaria and routed it. At the time, while the people to the north were wiped out for their terrible sins, the southern kingdom, under King Hezekiah, had been saved. This told the people of Judah that though their sins were many, they weren't "northern kingdom" many. Like the Pharisee, they prayed, "God, we thank You we aren't like other nations—especially like those nasty Samarians, or even worse, like Sodom back in the day."

What the people didn't realize was that, as time had progressed, their sins had exponentially increased. In fact, their level of wickedness had left the debauchery of Samaria, and even of Sodom, far behind. God proclaimed,

> "Your elder sister is Samaria, who dwells with her daughters to the north of you; and your younger sister, who dwells to the south of you, is Sodom and her daughters. You did not walk in their ways nor act according to their abominations; but, as if that were too little, you became

> more corrupt than they in all your ways. As I live," says the Lord GOD, "neither your sister Sodom nor her daughters have done as you and your daughters have done…Samaria did not commit half of your sins…You who judged your sisters, bear your own shame also, because the sins which you committed were more abominable than theirs; they are more righteous than you. Yes, be disgraced also, and bear your own shame, because you justified your sisters" (Ezekiel 16:46-48, 51-52).

There are many who will take passages like this and twist them into supposed evidence that God has abandoned Israel due to its sin. But that is only because they stop reading too soon. There is one principle we know about discipline prophecies against the Lord's people: Whenever we find a strong word against Israel, we won't have to look too far to find a balancing message of hope. Sometimes it is later in the book, and other times it is later in the chapter. This is one of those latter instances.

After laying out one of the harshest, most scathing parables condemning the people of Israel, the Lord God concluded by saying,

> Nevertheless I will remember My covenant with you in the days of your youth, and I will establish an everlasting covenant with you. Then you will remember your ways and be ashamed, when you receive your older and your younger sisters; for I will give them to you for daughters, but not because of My covenant with you. And I will establish My covenant with you. Then you shall know that I am the LORD, that you may remember and be ashamed, and never open your mouth anymore because of your shame, when I provide you an atonement for all you have done (verses 60-63).

God's covenant never fails. The Lord remains true to His word, and, thus, Israel will be restored. This was true for those in exile, and it was true when Israel became a nation once again in 1948.

"Okay, Amir, I get the forgiveness and all. But this doesn't read like there's a happy relationship between God and Israel." That's true, but that's because of the context. Remember the severity of the chapter. Coming back with "But it'll be all 'happy happy joy joy' when we're together again" would steal the oomph of the judgment that the Lord was communicating. If it's restoration "happy happy joy joy" you want, there are many places in Scripture you can find that message. In fact, Isaiah is chock-full of them.

> "Your Maker is your husband, the LORD of hosts is His name; and your Redeemer is the Holy One of Israel; He is called the God of the whole earth. For the LORD has called you like a woman forsaken and grieved in spirit, like a youthful wife when you were refused," says your God. "For a mere moment I have forsaken you, but with great mercies I will gather you. With a little wrath I hid My face from you for a moment; but with everlasting kindness I will have mercy on you," says the LORD, your Redeemer (Isaiah 54:5-8).

In the Ezekiel passage, we heard the hurt Husband. In Isaiah, we read the words of the forgiving and redeeming Lord. One God, two literary contexts, a near and a far view, and a single restored nation, eventually united eternally with the Father.

Riddle Me a Riddle (17)

Get ready for some literary fun. God told Ezekiel, "Son of man, pose a riddle, and speak a parable to the house of Israel" (Ezekiel 17:2). I'm sorry to say that every English translation I've seen of this passage has gotten this wonderful turn of phrase wrong. What was the prophet being asked to do for the house of Israel? He was told to "חוּד חִידָה וּמְשֹׁל מָשָׁל" (*chud chudah l'mashal mashal*). In English, God is telling him to "riddle a riddle and proverb a proverb." Oh, you folks really need to learn to speak Hebrew. It's such a wonderful language! A proverb and a riddle are brief puzzle stories that are best understood with a little bit of explanation. Thankfully, after presenting the word picture, the Lord graciously tells us what it means.

Here's the basic plot: A great eagle flew to Lebanon, where he took a cedar branch and planted it in a city of trade. The branch grew, but surprisingly, it turned into a vine. Another eagle came soaring in, and the vine liked its look. So it turned its back on the first eagle and reached for this new one instead. Not a good choice. As punishment for its disloyalty, the vine was pulled up by its roots, after which it withered and died.

On the surface, this seems like another story about God blessing Israel and Israel reaching for other gods instead. *Au contraire.* This tale takes us to kings and nations and treaties. The Lord began His explanation, saying:

> Indeed the king of Babylon went to Jerusalem and took its king and princes, and led them with him to Babylon. And he took the king's offspring, made a covenant with him, and put him under oath. He also took away the mighty of the land, that the kingdom might be brought low and not lift itself up, but that by keeping his covenant it might stand. But he rebelled against him by sending his ambassadors to Egypt, that they might give him horses and many people. Will he prosper? Will he who does such things escape? Can he break a covenant and still be delivered? (verses 12-15).

In that short explanation, we find four kings, one covenant, and one rebellion. The first king is easy to recognize—Nebuchadnezzar, the king of Babylon. In 597 BC, this first eagle made his second trip to Jerusalem, at which time he deposed the second king, the cedar branch, Israel's King Jeconiah. In his stead, the Babylonian placed the ex-king's uncle, Zedekiah, the third king who is also the vine, on the throne. Zedekiah promised to be a good little vassal, swearing an oath and making a covenant with Nebuchadnezzar. When the invading army returned to Babylon, they took with them the ex-king Jeconiah and a bunch of other exiles, including Ezekiel.

All went well for a while, but vassalship didn't wear well on Zedekiah. Earlier, Judah had driven away Assyria. Why couldn't it do the same with Babylon? To up their rebellion odds, Zedekiah sent ambassadors south to Egypt, a nation that was also getting tired of Babylon's bullying. There, they met with Pharaoh Hophra, the fourth king and the second eagle, who promised help.

That didn't go well with God. As Joshua and the Israelites learned when they made a treaty with the lying Gibeonites as they were conquering the Promised Land, a covenant is a covenant no matter who it's with (Joshua 9). If you break it, you will pay the price. In fact, David was forced to deal with the consequences of his predecessor, King Saul, breaking that very same treaty Joshua had made with the Gibeonites so many years before (2 Samuel 21:1-11). I've got no great love for the Gibeonites, but I'm encouraged by the depth of God's commitment to keeping one's word. That is what gives me hope for the future for my people, Israel, as well as for myself as a believing member of the church.

Because of King Zedekiah's treachery in breaking his covenant, God pronounced judgment.

> Thus says the Lord God: "As I live, surely My oath which he despised, and My covenant which he broke, I will

recompense on his own head. I will spread My net over him, and he shall be taken in My snare. I will bring him to Babylon and try him there for the treason which he committed against Me. All his fugitives with all his troops shall fall by the sword, and those who remain shall be scattered to every wind; and you shall know that I, the LORD, have spoken" (Ezekiel 17:19-21).

As we've already seen, Zedekiah was blinded after seeing his sons killed in front of him. In Babylon, he was tried. And in Babylon, he was imprisoned until his death.

The story doesn't end there, however. Remember, when there is bad news from God, you need only to read a little further to discover some hope. The Lord told Ezekiel that He Himself will plant a branch on the mountain height of Israel. The branch will take root, grow, and spread its branches wide enough for birds from all over to come dwell within them. He concluded by saying, "All the trees of the field shall know that I, the LORD, have brought down the high tree and exalted the low tree, dried up the green tree and made the dry tree flourish; I, the LORD, have spoken and have done it" (verse 24).

God will make the dry tree flourish. That did not happen immediately following the exile. Israel got its legs under itself again, but the people were always under the rule of one foreign king or another. It's only now with modern, post-Holocaust Israel that we are seeing the flourishing of the dry tree. And it will be only after the tribulation, when the millennium has begun and Christ is ruling from His throne in Jerusalem, that "all the trees of the field shall know that I, the LORD…have done it."

Individual Accountability (18)

Does God take pleasure in punishing people? Reading about the severity of God's judgments in Ezekiel, you could almost understand some people asking that question. It's that old "big stick" vision of God, where people picture Him watching the earth from His throne in heaven just hoping to spot someone sinning so that He can bop them on the head.

But the more we learn about the Lord, the more we see how far that is from the truth. In fact, in our next illustration, we read the Lord saying, "'Do I have any pleasure at all that the wicked should die?' says the Lord God, 'and not that he should turn from his ways and live?'" (Ezekiel 18:23). This point is so important that the Lord repeats it 15 chapters later, saying, "'As I live,' says the Lord God, 'I have no pleasure in the death of the wicked, but that the wicked turn from his way and live. Turn, turn from your evil ways! For why should you die, O house of Israel?'" (33:11)? God's desire is repentance, not punishment. That path to repentance and salvation was purchased at the extraordinarily high price of His own Son. If we receive punishment, it is only because we have rejected what God has offered us as a free gift.

The picture we now see in Ezekiel is centered on a proverb of the day, which stated, "The fathers have eaten sour grapes, and the children's teeth are set on edge" (18:2). The people were complaining that what they were experiencing wasn't fair. "Why are we having to pay the price of our parents' and grandparents' sins?" they wailed. "Each person should be judged only for what they do, and we haven't done anything compared to them!"

They did have some merit to their argument. Through Jeremiah, God foretold the coming judgment, saying, "I will hand them over to trouble, to all kingdoms of the earth, because of Manasseh the son of Hezekiah, king of Judah, for what he did in Jerusalem" (Jeremiah 15:4). It had been nearly 50 years since that vile king had died. Why was this generation suffering the ramifications of Manasseh leading the nation into the depths of idolatry and shedding so "much innocent blood, till he had filled Jerusalem from one end to another"

(2 Kings 21:16)? This became such a common complaint that even Jeremiah referenced it from Jerusalem when he prophesied:

> In those days they shall say no more: "The fathers have eaten sour grapes, and the children's teeth are set on edge." But every one shall die for his own iniquity; every man who eats the sour grapes, his teeth shall be set on edge (Jeremiah 31:29-30).

It is in the final sentence of Jeremiah's quote that we find the point of Ezekiel's prophecy. Ultimately, people are judged for what they do, not for what anyone else does. Once again, people are forgetting the nature of sin. If you sin and someone next to you sins even worse, what does that make you? A sinner.

In Ezekiel's passage, the Lord first talked of a righteous man. Avoiding sin and doing what is right, this man lived the holy life to which we are all called. Of this man, God said, "If he has walked in My statutes and kept My judgments faithfully—he is just; he shall surely live!" (Ezekiel 18:9).

But what if this guy had a son who was a bad guy? All the good stuff his dad did, the son did the opposite. Would the dad's righteousness cover the son's unrighteousness? Absolutely not! "He shall not live! If he has done any of these abominations, He shall surely die; His blood shall be upon him" (verse 13).

But what if the bad son had a good son himself? This good son did all the righteous things his grandfather did and his father didn't. Would this grandson be punished because of his dad's sinfulness? "He shall not die for the iniquity of his father; he shall surely live!" (verse 17).

This seems so basic to many of us, but understand that these people were living with a works-based mindset. Their worship of the pantheon of Mesopotamian gods was all based on mollifying the deities and trying to make them happy. That pattern of works-for-blessings slipped into their view of worshipping the Lord. "If we carry out the sacrifices that God wants, then He'll be happy. If we don't, He'll be mad and He'll take it out on generations of our people."

It is that "follow the rules because that's what God wants" mindset that led to the prophet Samuel telling King Saul, "To obey is better than sacrifice, and to heed than the fat of rams" (1 Samuel 15:22). Saul thought all God cared about was getting his offerings. Samuel told him, "No, He wants your heart. His desire is for your loving obedience, not your checklist compliance."

That's what God wants from all of us. He is not interested in our religious activities. It is our passionate love that He longs for—love that "[comes] from a pure heart, from a good conscience, and from sincere faith" (1 Timothy 1:5). If He has that from us, all the activity stuff will take care of itself.

The people of Israel didn't understand that the sins of the past generations were what set this judgment in motion. But the destruction that was coming upon Jerusalem had its origin as much in their current rebellion and idolatry as it did in anything that had taken place before.

A Worthless Monarchy (19)

A nation is only as good as its leaders. Strong, godly leadership most often will guide the citizenry to righteousness, obedience, and spiritual prosperity. For the flip side of that coin, we need only to look at all the monarchs of the northern kingdom and a majority of those in the south. A microcosm of this disparity can be seen in the tenures of King Hezekiah and that of his son, Manasseh. With Hezekiah on the throne, the nation once again became wealthy. The people sought out the Lord, and the nation experienced a divine salvation from the unstoppable steamroller of Assyria. Then came Manasseh. He was determined to be the anti-Hezekiah. All that his dad stood for and honored, Manasseh destroyed. He flooded the nation with idol worship and even offered his own children to the fire-god Molech. It's no wonder that under his reign the nation was conquered, and the king himself was taken away for a time to Babylon.

When God looked at Israel's recent rulers, what He saw resembled Manasseh much more than Hezekiah. The kings had taken an already-struggling nation and had run it into the ground. Now, the Lord took the opportunity to call them out in a lament in Ezekiel 19.

A lioness gave birth to cubs. One of those tiny felines stood out among the others, so she gave him special attention. He became strong but fell into a trap set by other nations. The young lion was taken in chains down to Egypt.

Although the lioness was heartbroken, she knew she couldn't succumb to her mourning. She took another of her cubs and trained it to be strong and a fighter. But this lion, too, was trapped by the surrounding nations. Rather than going to Egypt, this one was taken to Babylon.

All this makes for a sad story. There was so much potential in these lion cubs. But neither was wise enough to avoid the hunter's net, and thus, all their great potential went to waste.

Before we move to the rest of this funeral song, let's determine what God was talking about. It's not too difficult a code to decipher. The lioness is the nation of Judah. She took one of her own, Jehoahaz, and made him ruler over the people. In him was all that was needed to be the strong, fierce, godly king that the people required. Instead, "he did evil in the sight of the LORD" (2 Kings 23:32). As a result, after only three months, he fell into the trap of Pharaoh Necho, who "took Jehoahaz and went to Egypt, and [Jehoahaz] died there" (verse 34).

God bypassed the next king, Jehoiakim, and moved on to Jehoiachin, the son of Jehoiakim and the nephew of Jehoahaz. By the way, if you get a little confused with this final flurry of kings, it's totally understandable. Their names all sound similar in English. This is where it would have been nice if the Bible had come with a scorecard.

When we compare Jehoiachin with his uncle Jehoahaz, we can see why God skipped a monarch. Both kings were young when they took the throne—Jehoahaz was 23 and Jehoiachin was only 18. Like Jehoahaz, the younger Jehoiachin "did evil in the sight of the LORD, according to all that his father had done" (24:9). Each served the same very short duration, only three months. And both kings were taken captive and carried away to foreign lands, never to see Jerusalem again.

Such a sad story, but the Lord wasn't through. He had one more tale to tell, and this one was targeted right at King Zedekiah (Ezekiel 19:10-14). Instead of the mother being a lion this time, she was a vine, for us a familiar illustration of Israel by now. She was fruitful and strong, and from her branches were made scepters for kings. But then trouble came. She was uprooted from her lush garden and replanted in the desert. Her strong branches were snapped off and her fruit was destroyed. Worst of all, there was no wood strong enough to fashion a true scepter.

Imagine Zedekiah hearing this. Jeremiah had already told the monarch many times that his kingdom was going down in flames. Now, this new prophet in Babylon was preaching doom and gloom to all the people in exile, saying that Zedekiah wasn't made of strong enough stock to even be a king. He was a weak-sauce ruler in a broken and shattered nation. In five years' time, neither his throne nor Jerusalem would still be standing. So sad. Truly lamentable.

Vines, adulterous wives, eagles and branches, sour grapes, lions, and more vines. God used each of these pictures to illustrate the depths to which Israel had fallen and the heartbreak that it caused Him. I wish I could say that it gets cheerier from here onward, but I can't. The sin has been called out. Now it's time to witness the judgment.

CHAPTER 6

JUST HOW NASTY YOU ARE

EZEKIEL 20–24

Sin has consequences. Sadly, it is not always just the guilty ones who pay. In Ezekiel, we are confronted with a litany of wicked activities and their resulting punishments. People sin, and they get the just return for their actions. But what we can't miss are the others—the innocents, the righteous—who get caught up in the ensuing carnage. It's true there are times when God protects those who remain faithful to Him. We've already met three of them. Noah was saved from the worldwide flood. Daniel was removed from Jerusalem well before the worst of the violence and starvation of the siege-ravaged city. Then there was Job, who suffered incredible loss and pain because of an arrogant challenge from Satan himself. Although Job endured the worst, he was saved from death and recompensed greatly.

But there are many others who sustained great loss because of others' wickedness. Elijah sometimes lived on the run, pursued by the agents of a narcissistic king and a vengeful queen. At one point, he was physically sustained by food the Lord sent through helpful birds. And we can't forget Jeremiah, especially as we read of all the horrors that befell Jerusalem. He was a highly favored prophet doomed to live through a sinful city's judgment. Despite his faithfulness, he was beaten, mocked, thrown into a muddy pit, held in prison, and eventually dragged down to Egypt, the very place of which he had warned the people, "If you go down to Egypt, there you will meet your miserable ends." The last view we are given of this punching-bag prophet is in Pharaoh's land, prophesying, "Don't think we're safe here. On this very spot where I'm standing, Nebuchadnezzar is going to place his victorious army. And all except for a very small remnant of you are going to die here in this land." Judging by the silence following that prophecy, Jeremiah was one of those buried under the Egyptian sand.

Then we have Ezekiel. While he may have escaped the destruction of Jerusalem, his call as a prophet was not an easy one. In fact, in this chapter of our book, we will come to what—to me—is the most tragic and personal loss that any of God's spokesmen suffered in the line of duty. Throughout this section, and particularly when we come to that part in Ezekiel's story, we need to remember why it happened. It wasn't because of anything the prophet did wrong. In fact, he was faithfully serving God, and this was part of his service. If we're looking for a direction in which to point our finger of blame, there was a whole conclave of Jews transported to Babylon who were culpable for Ezekiel's tragedy because of the sins they had committed. And, even more so, there was still a population back in the holy city whose wickedness had finally pushed the Lord over the edge.

When we sin, it is typically not only us who pay the price. Iniquity is not so cut and dried. Our unrighteous choices can affect our spouse, our children, our church, our coworkers, our friends, and the list goes on. It would be so helpful if a ten-minute cooling-off period was required before we engaged in any sinful activity. Then we could think about the widespread fallout we could inflict on others or on our own relationship with God. Chances are a lot of stupidity could be averted that way.

But that's not how it works. Temptation comes, we drop our guard, then we're faced with trying to mitigate the damage. If only a simple consideration for the glory of God and the wonderful gift of salvation that He's given to us were enough to keep us from sin. Sometimes it is. But if reflecting on our salvation were 100 percent effective, then we would live sinlessly, and we know that doesn't happen (2 Chronicles 6:36; 1 John 1:8-10). It is through prayer, time in the Word, and life experience that we learn to use the ramifications of our sin as an encouragement to holiness.

A Clanging Gong (20)

Finally, you have a day off from work, but it hasn't turned out as you planned. Your wife has been at a day retreat with her friends, so you're home with your kid. You had been looking forward to this father/son time, but from the moment he got up, he's been a bear to deal with. In a foul mood, demanding, unappreciative, rude. Ask him to do something, and he ignores you. Tell him to put his lunch dishes away, and he loudly drops them in the sink, stalks back to his bedroom, and slams the door. *That's fine*, you think. *I had hoped for more, but I'm done with him for the day.*

Then, after a full morning and afternoon of passive-aggressive rebelliousness, your son surprises you by showing up with two mitts and a baseball. "Hey, Dad, want to go toss the ball around?"

Suddenly, you're faced with a choice. This is what you'd been hoping for from the time you first woke up. But by acquiescing to what he wants, wouldn't you be giving tacit approval of his behavior? As difficult as it is to say, you tell him, "There is nothing I want more than to play with you. But your behavior has been terrible. I'm not going to reward it. So, no, we will not be tossing the ball today." As your son storms away and once again slams his bedroom door, you sigh and tell yourself, *As disappointing as that was, it had to be done.*

The day was August 14, 591 BC, a little more than two years before

Nebuchadnezzar's siege of Jerusalem would begin. Ezekiel received some important visitors; the exiled elders of Israel were back. Once again, they came to inquire of the Lord God. They must have been thinking this was a spiritually good thing to do. Maybe they thought they were doing God a favor, including Him in their discussions. "It's been a while since we asked His opinion about anything. Maybe He's feeling a little left out of the important decisions."

Whether they voiced their question or not, we don't know because it is never mentioned. Instead, what we see is God essentially saying, "No, boys, we will not be tossing the ball today."

> Son of man, speak to the elders of Israel, and say to them, "Thus says the Lord GOD: 'Have you come to inquire of Me? As I live,' says the Lord GOD, 'I will not be inquired of by you'" (Ezekiel 20:3).

God then goes on to recite a full catalog of the sins of the people and of their fathers. Before He brought them out of Egypt, He had told them to cast away their idols, but they didn't (verses 3-8). When they were out of Egypt, He gave them the Sabbath, telling them to keep that day holy. But they didn't (verses 12-13). While they were in the wilderness, He gave them the law and told them to follow it, but they didn't (verses 18-21). Over and over, He had told them to change their ways or face the consequences, but they ignored Him. They even had the audacity to sacrifice their children by fire to appease their false gods (verses 23-26). Their whole history had been one of rebellion and idol worship and offering sacrifices to other gods in places other than the temple. One sin after another. Even while in exile, they hadn't changed.

> "So shall I be inquired of by you, O house of Israel? As I live," says the Lord GOD, "I will not be inquired of by

you. What you have in your mind shall never be, when you say, 'We will be like the Gentiles, like the families in other countries, serving wood and stone'" (verses 31-32).

I can't help but think of what Paul wrote to the Corinthians:

> Though I speak with the tongues of men and of angels, but have not love, I have become sounding brass or a clanging cymbal. And though I have the gift of prophecy, and understand all mysteries and all knowledge, and though I have all faith, so that I could remove mountains, but have not love, I am nothing. And though I bestow all my goods to feed the poor, and though I give my body to be burned, but have not love, it profits me nothing (1 Corinthians 13:1-3).

Love is a necessary ingredient if one is to effectively serve the Lord. Without it, you can preach all you want, prophesy all you want, give all you want, and sacrifice all you want, but it will be worthless. In God's ears, your words or actions are like a badly tuned trumpet or a brash-sounding cymbal.

These elders came with arrogant hearts believing that because they were asking God for insights, the Lord was obligated to answer them. Instead, God told them, "Your hearts are full of sin, as have been the hearts of your fathers for generations. Because of that, your 'humble' inquiries are like fingernails on a chalkboard. First, clean up your act; then maybe we'll talk."

A Glimpse of the Millennium (20)

What did I say earlier about the harshness of God's judgment? When it feels like He's done with Israel, keep reading. It'll get better. Like a ray of sunshine breaking through the storm clouds, the last part of Ezekiel 20 shines hope in the midst of condemnation. It reminds me of when God sent a beam of mercy into the midst of the sorrowful dirge of the book of Lamentations. As Jeremiah wept over the destruction of Jerusalem, he wrote these surprising words:

> This I recall to my mind, therefore I have hope. Through the Lord's mercies we are not consumed, because His compassions fail not. They are new every morning; great is Your faithfulness. "The Lord is my portion," says my soul, "Therefore I hope in Him!" (Lamentations 3:21-24).

The end of Ezekiel 20 is the Lamentations 3 of this litany of judgment. After promising a diaspora of Israel, the Lord reversed course and promised to bring the people back home. He would make the returning exiles "pass under the rod," a shepherding term that refers to a shepherd allowing into the pen those sheep that belong to him and rejecting those that don't.

> "For on My holy mountain, on the mountain height of Israel," says the Lord God, "there all the house of Israel, all of them in the land, shall serve Me; there I will accept them, and there I will require your offerings and the firstfruits of your sacrifices, together with all your holy things. I will accept you as a sweet aroma when I bring you out from the peoples and gather you out of the countries where you have been scattered; and I will be hallowed in you before the Gentiles. Then you shall know that I am the Lord, when I bring you into the land of Israel, into the country for which I raised My hand in an oath to give to your fathers. And there you shall remember your ways and all your doings with which you were defiled; and you shall loathe yourselves in your own sight because of all the

evils that you have committed. Then you shall know that I am the LORD, when I have dealt with you for My name's sake, not according to your wicked ways nor according to your corrupt doings, O house of Israel," says the Lord GOD (Ezekiel 20:40-44).

I included this entire quote because I want to make sure you get the full context. This did not happen when the Babylonian exiles returned home. As we saw earlier, Ezra and Nehemiah made it quite apparent that not every returnee would have "passed under the rod." The same is true for modern Israel. Something is going to have to happen that will change people's mindsets and return their loyalty to their Maker.

What we see in the above passage is a people who are a "sweet aroma" to the Lord, who through their commitment to God hallow Him before the onlooking Gentiles. On the mountain of Jerusalem, they will recognize their sins and loathe themselves for the evil they have committed. Put another way, "I will pour on the house of David and on the inhabitants of Jerusalem the Spirit of grace and supplication; then they will look on Me whom they pierced. Yes, they will mourn for Him as one mourns for his only son, and grieve for Him as one grieves for a firstborn" (Zechariah 12:10).

When you rebuff your son's manipulative attempt to play catch, you do so not with the mindset of permanently rejecting him. You are disciplining him, and you know very well that a day will come—hopefully as soon as tomorrow—when you will be back to tossing a ball around. But you'll be doing so with a young man who has learned an important lesson about respect and proper behavior.

The elders came to inquire of God, and He sent them away with harsh words and a demand for change. But He did so knowing that eventually, a time would come when a more mature, more righteous people would return to Him. They would be repentant of their old ways and ready to follow Him. In that day, not only will He listen to their inquiries, but He will fellowship with them as a Father does His children.

The Swinging of the Sword (21)

God's pronouncing of judgment against Israel continued. The illustration that He employed was His sword, which "shall go out of its sheath against all flesh from south to north, that all flesh may know that I, the Lord, have drawn My sword out of its sheath; it shall not return anymore" (Ezekiel 21:4-5). But amidst all the swordplay, with the blade being polished and sharpened then used for striking and cutting, God tasked Ezekiel with three visuals to emphasize His point.

First, the prophet was told to groan in sorrow for all to see.

> Sigh therefore, son of man, with a breaking heart, and sigh with bitterness before their eyes. And it shall be when they say to you, "Why are you sighing?" that you shall answer, "Because of the news; when it comes, every heart will melt, all hands will be feeble, every spirit will faint, and all knees will be weak as water. Behold, it is coming and shall be brought to pass," says the Lord God (verses 6-7).

This makes one wonder whether the exiles in these days leading up to the siege of Jerusalem were putting the city's coming destruction out of their thoughts. Judah was quite a distance away. Out of sight, out of mind. When they did think of it, the mileage gap may have caused them to downplay the impending violence. "Glad I'm not there. Probably won't be too fun for them," they'd say with an awkward chuckle before turning their attention back to their stew bowls.

But God wasn't pleased with the exiles' "stinks to be them" attitude. The people facing the onslaught were their families and friends and neighbors. The siege was coming, and the consequences to the city would be terrible. When the stories made it to Babylon, "every heart [would] melt...and all knees [would] be weak as water" (verse 7).

Sadly, it reminds me of the attitude that some in the church have toward those who will experience the tribulation. "That's going to be rough, but they really do deserve it. Hope they're good at dodging enormous hailstones," they say with an awkward chuckle before turning their attention back to their iPhones.

When we read in Revelation the details of what those seven years will be like, we must do so with our families, friends, and neighbors at the forefront of our minds. Taking time to visualize a loved one enduring the seals, trumpets, and bowls is enough to make anyone's heart melt and knees become weak as water.

Ezekiel's second action was to cry out and to strike his hands together (verses 12-14). Again, God wanted him to get the attention of the people so that they awakened from their apathy. If it wasn't for His grace in rescuing them from the coming doom, they would be facing the starvation, plague, and sword that was coming to the once-great city.

> I have set the point of the sword against all their gates, that the heart may melt and many may stumble. Ah! It is made bright; it is grasped for slaughter: swords at the ready! Thrust right! Set your blade! Thrust left—wherever your edge is ordered! (verses 15-16).

This was such a graphic description of the Babylonian soldiers flooding the streets of Jerusalem, swinging their swords right and left. The blades cut flesh and bone, dropping people to the ground. The lucky ones died outright from their wounds. The others slowly bled out as the carnage continued. The Lord was reminding Ezekiel's listeners, "This could have been you, exiles. You could have felt that cold steel as it plunged into your bodies and stole away your life."

The third task given to Ezekiel was to provide a demonstration of a decision that King Nebuchadnezzar would have to make. The prophet was to create a road then have it split into a *Y*. At the point of divergence, he was to place a sign that reads "Judah" with an arrow pointing one way, and "Ammon" with an arrow pointing the other way.

When enough people had gathered and wondered what the young, weird prophet was doing, Ezekiel would explain that Nebuchadnezzar and his army were going to stop when they arrived at the fork in the road. To decide whether he would head toward Jerusalem in Judah or Rabbah of the Ammonites, he would turn to various forms of divination. The Lord would ensure that the signs the king sought would all point to Jerusalem. It was that city's time to go, and God was sending the Babylonians to make certain that every structure would be destroyed, including His temple.

Nebuchadnezzar would then build his siege mound and set up his battering rams, just like Ezekiel had demonstrated earlier with the drawing on the clay brick. Despite the overwhelming size of the army, many of the people in the city would think that God was going to divinely rescue them, just as He had done when the Assyrians came knocking back in King Hezekiah's day. But not this time.

> Now to you, O profane, wicked prince of Israel, whose day has come, whose iniquity shall end, thus says the Lord GOD: "Remove the turban, and take off the crown; nothing shall remain the same. Exalt the humble, and humble the exalted. Overthrown, overthrown, I will make it overthrown! It shall be no longer, until He comes whose right it is, and I will give it to Him" (verses 25-27).

Two observations about that statement. First, the use of repetition is powerful and definitive. Saying something three times emphasizes the absolute nature of the word. Think of the seraphim hovering over the throne of God, crying out, "Holy, holy, holy is the LORD of hosts...!" (Isaiah 6:3). The Lord is absolutely, completely, 100 percent the perfection of holiness. So when we read, "Overthrown, overthrown, I will make it overthrown!," it is clear that Jerusalem is about to be utterly, completely, and thoroughly decimated.

The second observation is another sunbeam breaking through the storm clouds. Look at Ezekiel's last sentence in the above passage. Who is "He"? The capitalized letter kind of gives it away. Jerusalem was rebuilt after the exile, but never to its ultimate glory. Even with the incredible growth after statehood in the twentieth and twenty-first centuries, the city pales in comparison to what it will become. Once the rightful King sits on the throne after His return at the second coming, only then will Jerusalem achieve its full glory.

One last item: What about Rabbah of Ammon? Did the people there dodge a bullet when Nebuchadnezzar turned toward Judah? No, their destruction was simply delayed. The last part of chapter 21 tells us that once the sword was done with Jerusalem, it was Ammon-bound, with predictable results.

Bloody, Drossy, Worthless Leaders (22)

Once more, the Lord turned His attention to the king, the princes, and the leaders of Judah. He began generally, calling out the city for its spilling of blood. "Now, son of man, will you judge, will you judge the bloody city? Yes, show her all her abominations" (Ezekiel 22:2). The people of the city shed blood, made idols, and defiled themselves with those same idols. In fact, they did it to such a degree that they became a laughingstock to the nations around them. God said they "mock you as infamous and full of tumult" (verse 5).

Then God narrowed it down. Earlier, we talked about how a city is only as good as its leaders. Never was this truer than in Jerusalem. The royalty of the city were trashy, violent people, according to God. "Look, the princes of Israel: each one has used his power to shed blood in you" (verse 6). The Lord proceeded to voice a litany of sins committed by those who should be leading the people toward righteousness. Instead, they were violent, mockers of their parents, oppressors of strangers, mistreaters of orphans and widows, profaners of the holy, committers of lewd acts with anyone they could find including family members, takers of bribes, usurers, and extorters. It's quite the list, but it fits the bill. The whole catalog of sins can be attributed to one reason that the Lord gave at the end of the succession of shame. "'[They] have forgotten Me,' says the Lord GOD" (verse 12).

When God is our focus, we have a supernatural "temptation protector" in the Holy Spirit, who allows us to know when the enemy is trying to bring us down. However, when we forget God and turn away from Him, then we quench that warning bell of the Holy Spirit. This opens us up to the devil's wily ways. That's the very reason the apostle Peter warned, "Be sober, be vigilant; because your adversary the devil walks about like a roaring lion, seeking whom he may devour" (1 Peter 5:8).

I watched a YouTube video recently of a young child at a zoo. His back was to a large glass window, behind which spread a large cat exhibit. While he toddled and shuffled, waiting for his parents to take his picture, an enormous tiger skulked over a rise a number of meters behind him. It spotted the boy and crouched. Slowly, it began to creep forward, one inaudible step at a time. Meanwhile, the child was laughing and dancing for his parents, totally oblivious to what was taking place. The tiger took a few more steps, then it lunged. People nearby who were watching the scene cried out, causing the little boy to run crying to his parents. The disappointed tiger, having once again been reminded by the glass that he was not in the wild anymore, moped away.

This is a picture of our spiritual life. We are the little boy, the tiger is the devil and his minions, and the protective glass is the Holy Spirit. Unfortunately, there are times when, through a lack of prayer, time in the Word, and fellowship with other believers, we allow our glass to become paper thin. Or, through outright rebellion against God, much like the "princes of Israel" (Ezekiel 22:6), we drop the barrier entirely. I can't imagine what that tiger would have done to the child if the glass hadn't been there, but I do know it is exactly what Satan wants to do to our walk with the Lord. We must be diligent!

This abandonment of God by the princes of Israel, and thus the people of Israel, was such a disappointment to God. He had provided so much for them. They had everything they needed to be His light to the world and to live a blessed life. But rather than living in a manner beautiful to the surrounding nations, they were nothing more than ugly refuse. Instead of shining like precious metals, "the house of Israel has become dross to Me; they are all bronze, tin, iron, and lead, in the midst of a furnace; they have become dross from silver" (verse 18). Scum, dross, slag—the once-beautiful Israel of Solomon's day that drew in visitors from nations far and wide had become useless waste. And it was all because of the people's individual choices to turn their backs to God and their faces toward idolatry and wickedness. To this nation, the Lord pronounced His verdict, saying, "As silver is melted in the midst of a furnace, so shall you be melted in its midst; then you shall know that I, the LORD, have poured out My fury on you" (verse 22).

But the Lord was still not done with His condemnation, particularly as it was directed toward the leadership of the nation. In the rest of this chapter, God called out the groups of authority figures who had led the people into sin. He went after the prophets, the priests, the princes, and then the prophets once again. He cited the same inventory of sins He had presented before. Concluding this prophecy, God said:

> The people of the land have used oppressions, committed robbery, and mistreated the poor and needy; and they

wrongfully oppress the stranger. So I sought for a man among them who would make a wall, and stand in the gap before Me on behalf of the land, that I should not destroy it; but I found no one. Therefore I have poured out My indignation on them; I have consumed them with the fire of My wrath; and I have recompensed their deeds on their own heads (verses 29-31).

As the leaders led, so the people followed. The Lord searched for one leader who would stand in the gap to divert the coming wrath. Was there not one man who had the righteousness, character, and position to turn the people around? Sadly, no. God did have a remnant, but none of those who still turned their eyes toward Him had the authority to make a difference. Therefore, the city and the present form of the monarchy were doomed.

Sisters, Sisters (23)

As I thought about writing this book, there were many considerations that excited me very much. The greatest of which was having the opportunity to fully flesh out the return of Israel in chapters 34, 36, and 37, and to dive deep into what I believe is the not-too-distant-future war found in chapters 38 and 39. On the other hand, there were a few sections that I was dreading, two of which are found in chapters 23 and 24. The first one is icky, and the second one is painful.

You may have had the same experience that many other couples have had. A friend recommends to you some new, amazing series on Netflix or some other streaming service. They can't stop raving about it, so you decide to give it a try with your spouse. But as soon as you turn it on, you see the TV-MA rating up in the top corner. Often it includes the reasons for its mature-audiences-only rating—"profanity, nudity, sexuality, violence." You and your spouse look at each other, sigh, then press the "Off" button and pick up a book.

Chapter 23 is the only chapter of the Bible onto which I would affix a TV-MA rating. Or, if it was playing in a theater, I'd assign it as NC-17. Thankfully, the translators of the NKJV softened the wording so you have to read between the lines in certain sections—not that you'd want to. If you read this chapter in the ESV or NIV, the shocking details are there in all their glory.

This is the story of two sisters. The older sister, Oholah, represented Samaria, capital of the northern kingdom. The younger sister, Oholibah, was the southern kingdom's capital, Jerusalem. Neither were the kind of girls you'd want your sons to bring home for dinner on family night. Oholah quickly fell into the ways of adultery. She slept around with the Assyrians until they tired of her and killed her. Not good. Clear and important lesson. Right, little sister?

Rather than taking a clue about the potential negative results of living an adulterous lifestyle, Oholibah thought, *Whatever big sis can do, I can do better*. She started looking for lovers wherever she could find them. The list is long, and the description is very graphic. Ultimately, Oholibah found herself in the same destroyed and dispersed state as her sister, Oholah. Their stories were to be a testament to all the citizens of Jerusalem of their own whoring ways. And they were to specifically be a warning to the women of Israel to stop their disgustingly immoral lifestyles. As the Lord said, wrapping up this chapter:

> Thus I will cause lewdness to cease from the land, that all women may be taught not to practice your lewdness. They shall repay you for your lewdness, and you shall pay for your idolatrous sins. Then you shall know that I am the Lord God (Ezekiel 23:48-49).

"You've been gross. Now you're going to pay for your sins." With that chapter dealt with, I'm now going to go out on my patio, sip a triple-shot espresso, stare at the beauty of the Jezreel Valley, and think happy thoughts.

The Beginning of the End (24)

The day was January 15, 588 BC. Two occurrences took place that day. One was important to Jerusalem and the other to Ezekiel. Together, they were momentous enough that the prophet began his next prophecy with a date stamp.

> Again, in the ninth year, in the tenth month, on the tenth day of the month, the word of the LORD came to me, saying, "Son of man, write down the name of the day, this very day—the king of Babylon started his siege against Jerusalem this very day" (Ezekiel 24:1-2).

The beginning of the end had begun. The final siege of the once-great city by Nebuchadnezzar had commenced. The annals of the kings confirm this date:

> Now it came to pass in the ninth year of his reign, in the tenth month, on the tenth day of the month, that Nebuchadnezzar king of Babylon and all his army came against Jerusalem and encamped against it; and they built a siege wall against it all around (2 Kings 25:1).

Ninth year, tenth month, tenth day, Nebuchadnezzar launched the attack that would gradually destroy the city in which God had placed His house. But even as the siege walls went up, King Zedekiah and the elders of Israel told the people that they needn't worry. "We're safe, everyone! Look at our magnificent walls! These walls are like an iron pot, and we are like meat safe inside. Besides, we've got God. Just wait for Him to act like He's done before!"

But as we've seen in the previous 23 chapters of Ezekiel's prophecies, the situation had changed since the days of Hezekiah. The leaders of Israel were scoundrels, and the people were idolatrous rebels. God was not on Jerusalem's side anymore. To the leaders' words of hope, the Lord replied, "You think you're safe, like a choice cut of meat in a pot? Think again. You may be like a piece of meat, but the fire is going to burn so hot on the pot and so long that you're going to turn to ash. Then I'm going to burn the pot too."

> Heap on the wood, kindle the fire; cook the meat well, mix in the spices, and let the cuts be burned up. Then set the pot empty on the coals, that it may become hot and its bronze may burn, that its filthiness may be melted in it, that its scum may be consumed (Ezekiel 24:10-11).

The princes and leaders displayed an arrogant, uninformed attitude. In their minds, God was simply a big, burly, obedient bodyguard. But they had it all backwards. God is the One in control. He gives us our freedom to live and act as we want. But our freedom is like a rope attached to our necks. There is only so far we can go before we will either turn back to God or keep going and hang ourselves.

Now we come to the incident that I mentioned at the beginning of this chapter as the most tragic personal loss of any prophet.

> The word of the LORD came to me, saying, "Son of man, behold, I take away from you the desire of your eyes with one stroke; yet you shall neither mourn nor weep, nor shall your tears run down. Sigh in silence, make no mourning for the dead; bind your turban on your head, and put your sandals on your feet; do not cover your lips, and do not eat man's bread of sorrow." So I spoke to the people

in the morning, and at evening my wife died; and the next morning I did as I was commanded (verses 15-18).

I can't read that without my eyes misting up. As I mentioned before, my writing partner, Pastor Rick, knows what it's like to be told that his wife is going to die. He and his beloved Linda were in a doctor's office when they heard her diagnosis of terminal esophageal cancer. It was a blow, but there were two gifts Rick had that Ezekiel did not. First, he and Linda had those final months together, which he wouldn't trade for anything. Second, he knew that her departure was just part of life. They were in their eighties, and they knew that for both of them, the day would come sooner rather than later. This didn't make the situation easier, but it made it understandable.

Ezekiel was barely in his thirties. One morning when he met with God, the Lord told him that his wife was going to die. That same evening, she was gone. Why? Because God wanted to make a point to the people. Apparently, sending a memo or eating some more dung-cooked bread wasn't enough to communicate what He wanted to say. God had determined that the best way to illustrate His prophecy was to take the life of the prophet's beloved partner. This was wonderful for her because she got to see her God. It was horrible for Ezekiel because he lost the apple of his eye. What point could be that important?

It was this: Just like Ezekiel's wife was his delight, the temple in Jerusalem was the delight of God. However, it was also the delight of the people of the exile. As long as it stood, the sinful population had a tangible demonstration of their supposedly strong connection to God. The day was soon coming, though, when they would get word that the temple had fallen. "Just know," God told them, "that I was behind that."

> Thus says the Lord God: "Behold, I will profane My sanctuary, your arrogant boast, the desire of your eyes,

the delight of your soul; and your sons and daughters whom you left behind shall fall by the sword" (verse 21).

This reminds me of Jesus' powerful words, "Therefore My Father loves Me, because I lay down My life that I may take it again. No one takes it from Me, but I lay it down of Myself" (John 10:17-18). This temple wouldn't be destroyed because of the will of Nebuchadnezzar, but because of the will of God. No one can take anything from the Lord, be it the life of His Son or the temple of His name that He placed in Jerusalem.

God told the people that when the day came and the temple was destroyed, they shouldn't mourn for it—just as Ezekiel didn't mourn for his wife. They had brought this on themselves. They were suffering the just punishment for their sins. It was time for them to turn things around so that the Lord could turn the page and begin the next chapter for Israel.

CHAPTER 7

BLAST RADIUS

EZEKIEL 25-28

The day was August 4, 2020. In the city of Beirut, a fire began in a warehouse in the port district. Seven years earlier, a Molodovan-flagged freighter, MV *Rhosus*, made temporary port in Beirut. The primary cargo it carried was 2,750 metric tons of highly explosive ammonium nitrate bound for Mozambique. The load was heavy, the provenance of the cargo was shady, and the financing of the journey was sparse. When the captain decided to load an additional shipment of heavy machinery to boost his meager profit, the structural integrity of the vessel was seriously damaged. With a ship no longer seaworthy, the owner of the *Rhosus* went bankrupt, the officers abandoned the ship and fled home, and the crew that had been stranded on board quickly ran out of provisions. With fees mounting, the port authority seized the cargo and transferred it to Warehouse 12. In 2018, the emptied freighter sank in the harbor.

At some point, in an act of logical incoherence, someone determined that it made perfect sense to store a very large stash of fireworks alongside the warehouse filled with the highly explosive compound. I mean, what could go wrong? Then, on that fateful summer day in 2020, a small fire blew up some of the fireworks. About 30 seconds later, a second explosion took place, and this one was massive. In Israel and Jordan to the south, people felt the blast, as did others in Syria to the east and Turkey to the north. On the island of Cyprus, 150 miles west in the Mediterranean Sea, some actually heard the detonation. In the countless eyewitness videos, you can watch the concussive wave tear through the city, flattening building after building. Two-hundred-and-eighteen people lost their lives, while another 700 were injured. The financial cost exceeded $15 billion. Logically, only a small handful of the dead could have possibly been part of the insane decision to store fireworks and ammonium nitrate together. But that didn't matter. When the blast was triggered, everyone in its radius succumbed to the wave.

Israel was not well-loved across the Fertile Crescent and down what is now called the Levant. At first the Hebrews were separatists, acting high and mighty and looking down on their new neighbors. "Our God is the only true God, so keep your cheap, knockoff idols away." But over a short amount of time, a bizarre turnaround took place. They dove deep into idol worship. Almost too deep, like the obnoxious kid who always tries too hard to prove himself. The people of Israel would say, "Oh, so you offered two kids to Molech? Well, I offered three." That kind of obnoxiousness made others want to beat up Israel, but the nation had a bully God who would sometimes step in and wipe out a whole army just for looking at His people wrong. So the surrounding nations watched and waited for the day when Israel would get its comeuppance.

Finally, it happened. In 586 BC, Nebuchadnezzar's army broke through the walls of Jerusalem and the city was razed to the ground. All the surrounding nations danced around and shouted for joy. Finally, those obnoxious Jews were gone. What the celebraters didn't realize, however, was that while the explosion of God's judgment was triggered in Jerusalem, its blast radius expanded in every direction. Israel may have been the chief of sinners, but righteousness is not a sliding scale. You either are righteous or you aren't. And, if you aren't, you can expect God's judgment, especially if you're dancing over the graves of His people.

The Other Nations

If you follow my Telegram channel or watch my videos, you will be familiar with the phrase, "God only talks about other nations as they relate to Israel." During the time of the Babylonian Empire, there were other thriving civilizations around the world. The Zhou Dynasty was all-powerful in China, the Etruscans were laying the foundations for the development of Rome, and the Celts were showing dominance in parts of Europe. Yet none of these strong people groups are mentioned in the Bible. Why? They had no contact with God's chosen nation. The Bible is the story of God's peoples—Israel and the church.

This left tens of millions of people outside the narrative of Scripture. But proximity brought many other nations in. In Ezekiel, God now turned His attention toward them. Yes, His primary focus was on His sinful people because He wanted to draw them back to Himself. However, there were many surrounding peoples who either contributed to Israel's delinquency or kicked the weakened nation when it was down. They had to answer for their sins. This was true even of those in Babylon, whom God used to carry out His punishment. However, despite their accomplishing God's plan, they certainly weren't doing it to please Him.

> "Call together the archers against Babylon. All you who bend the bow, encamp against it all around; let none of them escape. Repay her according to her work; according to all she has done, do to her; for she has been proud against the Lord, against the Holy One of Israel. Therefore her young men shall fall in the streets, and all her men of war shall be cut off in that day," says the Lord (Jeremiah 50:29-30).

Babylon was like a vicious attack dog on the end of God's leash. The Lord didn't need to coax Nebuchadnezzar and his armies to attack. That was their nature. It's what they did. So all God needed to do was to aim the attack dog in the right direction, unhook his restraint, and let him carry out the destruction he had already been planning. Again, the Lord's primary target was Judah, but, while He had Babylon at the end of his tether, He might as well use the wild beast to mete out some well-deserved punishment on some very sinful nations.

Judgment Against Ammon (25)

The Ammonites were located northeast of Jerusalem, across the Jordan River. Their capital was Rabbah, which is modern-day Amman, the capital of Jordan. When Abraham's nephew Lot escaped the destruction of Sodom by fleeing into the hills, he became isolated with his daughters. Fearing they might never have children in their hermitage hideaway, Lot's daughters devised a cringy plan to get pregnant through their father. The plan worked and the brothers/cousins Ammon and Moab were born. By the time the Hebrews made it back to the Promised Land after four centuries in Egypt, any connection between Lot's progeny and Abraham's was long gone.

By the way, it's easy for historical numbers to become a blur. Realize that the amount of time between Jacob's family going to Egypt and Moses leading them out is equivalent to the time between the pilgrims landing at Plymouth Rock and today. Four hundred years is a very, very long time. When the Hebrews came back to the Promised Land, it was filled with well-established kingdoms and city-states that had never heard of Abraham or Isaac or Jacob, and they had no idea what these vagabonds had in mind as they traveled up the wilderness roads to their land. Soon, they would learn the hard lesson that for the last several hundred years, they had merely been squatters on land that belonged to someone else.

It was back in Ezekiel 21 that we first heard that Ammon was in trouble. Now, God spelled out more clearly the cause for their punishment.

> Thus says the Lord God: "Because you said, 'Aha!' against My sanctuary when it was profaned, and against the land of Israel when it was desolate, and against the house of Judah when they went into captivity, indeed, therefore, I will deliver you as a possession to the men of the East, and they shall set their encampments among you and make their dwellings among you; they shall eat your fruit, and they shall drink your milk. And I will make Rabbah a stable for camels and Ammon a resting place for flocks. Then you shall know that I am the Lord" (Ezekiel 25:3-5).

Because of the familial relationship, as distant as it was, the people of Ammon should have at least mourned the plight of the northern kingdom of Israel and that of Judah in the south. Instead, they cheered it. They mocked it. God said, "You clapped your hands, stamped your feet, and rejoiced in heart with all your disdain for the land of Israel" (verse 6). It's bad enough to not help someone when they are down, but to mock them and celebrate their sorrow is just plain cruel.

Understanding that truth has kept me from losing myself in the sorrow and depression natural to the war my nation has been in. While my prayer is for strong justice to be carried out against the perpetrators of the terrorist violence, I still force myself to pray for the salvation of our enemies. This especially challenged me in March 2025, when a new Syrian regime led by former al-Qaeda member Ahmed al-Sharaa began slaughtering the Alawite minority who lived along the Mediterranean coastal areas. The Alawites were the people of Bashar al-Assad, the Syrian president who for years wanted nothing more than to destroy Israel. But now the legitimized terrorists of al-Sharaa's new Syrian army were humiliating Alawites by forcing them to walk on hands and knees and bark like dogs, torturing them by beating them with heavy rods and by using other more pointy objects, and then shooting them in the head. Sometimes they killed the rest of the family, too, just for fun.

My place was not to pick up a rifle and fight for these enemies of my country. However, I could use my social media platform to get out this story that the mainstream media was quashing because President al-Sharaa was their new darling. Those of you who follow my Telegram account and subscribe to my YouTube channel know the loud voice that I had determined to be for the helpless Alawites. As Jesus told us in the Sermon on the Mount, "Love your enemies, bless those who curse you, do good to those who hate you, and pray for those who spitefully use you and persecute you" (Matthew 5:44). That is our calling as believers, but it certainly was not how the Ammonites lived.

Because of the Ammonites' sins, God promised to them that He would "give you as plunder to the nations; I will cut you off from the peoples, and I will cause you to perish from the countries; I will destroy you, and you shall know that I am the Lord" (verse 7).

Judgment Against Moab (25)

Now it's time to deal with the other brother/cousin, Moab. Interestingly, it seems like God is a little less harsh in His punishment of this son of Lot's older daughter. Over the years, Moab and Israel had experienced mostly bad times, but there were a few good. During a famine in Israel, a family from Bethlehem fled to Moab for relief, which was located below Ammon, along the east side of the Dead Sea. After losing her husband and two sons, the matriarch of the family, Naomi, returned home, bringing her daughter-in-law, Ruth, who was a Moabite. Soon, Ruth married Boaz, and in the third generation of this union, King David was born. So even in the royal line of Israel there was a touch of Moabite blood. Later, when David was fleeing from King Saul, he stashed his parents away with the king of Moab for safekeeping (1 Samuel 22:3-4).

Now, many years after, what Moab had forgotten was that there was a special relationship between the Israelites and God. "The house of Judah is like all the nations," they claimed (verse 8). But Israel wasn't like all the nations, and that was a lesson Moab needed to be taught. Thus, God determined to "execute judgments upon Moab, and they shall know that I am the LORD" (verse 11).

Judgment Against Edom (25)

While Abraham's nephew, Lot, was having his own genetically questionable grandsons, Abraham also had a couple grandkids. His son, Isaac, married Rebekah, and they had twins, Esau and Jacob. Because of God's will and wisdom, He chose the younger son, Jacob, to carry Abraham's chosen line. Esau moved east toward Moab and Ammon, who were his uncles/cousins of one sort or another, settling farther south below the Dead Sea. The red dirt of the land was perfect for Esau, whose name means "red."

From the time of the twins' birth, Esau and Jacob didn't get along. Nothing changed over the ensuing generations. When Moses and company asked for permission to pass through Edom's land during the wilderness wandering, the Edomites said no. Many centuries later, when Israel was in desperate straits against Babylon, the people of Edom saw it as an opportunity to express their long-pent-up anger. They took "vengeance" on the house of Judah, "avenging itself" on them (verse 12).

The punishment meted out against Edom is interesting. Rather than having the forces of Babylon destroy the people, God said, "I will lay My vengeance on Edom by the hand of My people Israel, that they may do in Edom according to My anger and according to

My fury; and they shall know My vengeance" (verse 14). This is hard to fathom. Israel was itself under the disciplinary hand of God. How could they bring justice to the Edomites? Dr. Charles Dyer postulated,

> Edom was conquered by the Nabateans during the intertestamental period. The remnant of the Edomites (also called Idumeans) moved west to the Negev. Later they were forced to become Jewish converts (Josephus, *The Antiquities of the Jews* 13. 9. 1). Thus the Edomites lost both their country and their national identity.[4]

Vengeance on Edom was brought about indirectly through the people of Israel—God can be creative in His methods of judgment and of blessing. We may not know how or when He will bring about what is due. What we do know is that one way or another, because of His justice and His holiness, wickedness will always be punished, and righteousness will always be rewarded.

Judgment Against Philistia (25)

Now we come to the dreaded Philistines, the enemy in so many childhood Bible stories. Originally, they were part of a sea people known as the Phoenicians, but some of them settled down along the Mediterranean seacoast, much of which is now part of Israel. Eventually, they moved east up into the lower hills, and that was where most of the back-and-forth between the Philistines and Israel took place.

The judgment God pronounced against Philistia was similar to that given to Edom. "You hated my people, so you took vengeance against them whenever you had a chance." God promised strong punishment against them, but, as always, there was a purpose. "And they shall know that I am the LORD, when I lay My vengeance upon them" (verse 17). For too long, all the nations had said that Israel's God was dead, or that He could be defeated just like any one of their idol gods.

That era of lies was almost done. It was time that all knew who God was and the incredible power He had in the palms of His hands.

An Intro to Tyre (26)

At the risk of offending numerous readers, I am going to come out and admit that Las Vegas is not my favorite city. Despite some strong churches and many wonderful people, there is a layer of smarm that covers the town. It is a land of vice and hedonism, and I have great respect for those who feel the call and have the strength to remain and minister in Sin City.

Suppose I were to say to you, "In three years, Las Vegas will be no more. The whole city, good and bad alike, will be destroyed, and the memory of that intemperate oasis in the desert will fade into obscurity." Your response may be, "Wow, Amir, lighten up! Maybe you need another cappuccino." To which I would respond, "Great idea! I could always use another cappuccino. But that doesn't change the fact that in three years, there will be no *viva* left in Las Vegas."

At that point, you may just write me off as a kook. However, that would likely change if two years and eleven months later some catastrophic event took place and suddenly Las Vegas was no more and the whole area became uninhabitable. Instead of kook, suddenly you would call me a great man and a prophet. Now, before readers in Las Vegas start putting "For Sale" signs in their front yards, let me remind you that this is just an illustration. As the head of a "non-prophet" organization, I am legally forbidden from predicting the future.

Ezekiel was in a different situation. He was a prophecy-producing powerhouse who was about to drop a prediction that, when fulfilled, would have everyone stunned into the recognition that the Lord truly is God.

From all appearances, the city of Tyre was invincible. Divided into two parts, the mainland portion of the city was located about 12 miles north of Israel's border. The island section was located about

600 yards from the coast in the Mediterranean Sea. Together, the vista of the city was stunning, causing Ezekiel to write, "O Tyre, you have said, 'I am perfect in beauty.' Your borders are in the midst of the seas. Your builders have perfected your beauty" (27:3-4). Like a model strutting down a catwalk, Tyre knew she was gorgeous, as did everyone who looked at her.

Not only was Tyre nice to look at, she was rich too. The city had two ports into which ships from all over the Mediterranean and beyond would bring their wares. After unloading their cargo, they would fill up with their purchases from other ships' imports, then take their treasures back home. But it wasn't just import/export that made Tyre wealthy. Logs fashioned from Lebanese cedars were floated out from the city. The city also produced a rich purple dye made from mollusks, which could only be afforded by the richest of the rich. One gram of Tyrian dye was valued at 20 grams of gold.

Riches, strength, beauty—what more could a city want?

Humility. That's what was lacking in Tyre. You could have the most beautiful woman in the world sitting across the table from you, but the moment she says, "Look at me, I'm the most beautiful woman in the world," most guys I know would be asking for the check. Well, at least the guys who are able to get over the fact that they are somehow sitting across the table from the most beautiful woman in the world, which I'm guessing would greatly decrease the percentage. Men will be men, which is likely why, despite her obnoxious arrogance, Tyre was still the hot spot of the eastern Mediterranean coast.

There was one more sin of Tyre that was more Israel-centric, which is why their judgment fits into this series. Tyre was a city of sea wealth—goods transported by ship. A second type of wealth at the time was land wealth—goods transported by caravan. Because of the great Sahara Desert, if you wanted to move anything between Asia and Africa, it had to pass through a narrow strip of land that, like Tyre, was also along the eastern coast of the Mediterranean. That was the land of Israel. So, while Tyre had control of the sea traffic, Jerusalem controlled the caravan traffic.

But, once Jerusalem fell, oversight of the highways through the land became sketchy. Banditry grew. Merchants began to wonder whether it was safe enough to attempt a ground journey. Maybe it was worth the extra money to pay for water passage. The ship owners of Tyre were standing by to tell the merchants, "Step right up, my friends! Have we got the boat for you!" As we read in the word that the Lord gave to Ezekiel:

> It came to pass in the eleventh year, on the first day of the month, that the word of the LORD came to me, saying, "Son of man, because Tyre has said against Jerusalem, 'Aha! She is broken who was the gateway of the peoples; now she is turned over to me; I shall be filled; she is laid waste'" (26:1-2).

Jerusalem's loss was Tyre's gain. It's good to be the winner.

Notice that Ezekiel gave another time stamp. While the readers of the time would know exactly when the prophet was talking about, the fact that he neglected to include for us a month means we can only speculate as to the exact time of year. However, the eleventh year of Jehoiakim's exile is also when Jerusalem fell, so it is likely that this prophecy is connected to that event. What we gain by Ezekiel affirming the year of his prophecy is that now, no one can look back and say that the Lord's words spoken against Tyre were given at some later date. Instead, it's like he wrote out the prophecy, nailed it to the city gate for all to see, and let it hang there until the day it was finally and perfectly fulfilled. Then the people would know that the Lord is God.

The Judgment Against Tyre (26)

Because Tyre was such a great city with enormous wealth and far-reaching economic connections, it wasn't enough to just let Babylon come and destroy it. God wanted the arrogant inhabitants of the city to feel the spurning and degradation of all those in countries that once called them friends.

> Therefore thus says the Lord God: "Behold, I am against you, O Tyre, and will cause many nations to come up against you, as the sea causes its waves to come up. And they shall destroy the walls of Tyre and break down her towers; I will also scrape her dust from her, and make her like the top of a rock. It shall be a place for spreading nets in the midst of the sea, for I have spoken," says the Lord God; "it shall become plunder for the nations. Also her daughter villages which are in the fields shall be slain by the sword. Then they shall know that I am the Lord" (verses 3-6).

This puts us in a bit of a timeline conundrum. If this was to happen right away, then what would make Tyre different than any other bug that Nebuchadnezzar's giant army squashed underfoot? Especially because we know that the great king and his Babylonian fighting force did score a great victory against Tyre. Through Ezekiel, God said, "Behold, I will bring against Tyre from the north Nebuchadnezzar king of Babylon, king of kings, with horses, with chariots, and with horsemen, and an army with many people" (verse 7). When the king came, he came with *great* success. But he didn't come with *complete* success.

Following his thorough destruction of Jerusalem in 586 BC, Nebuchadnezzar turned north. After taking time to replenish, Babylon swept down against Tyre the next year, beginning a siege that would last for 13 years. The people trapped on the mainland suffered greatly and that part of the city was ultimately demolished. But water is a strong defense, and with Babylon being planted near the center of modern Iraq, it hadn't spent a lot of time building up a navy. So the island portion of Tyre survived, receiving supplies from the water out of reach of the Babylonian forces.

Some say that there was an eventual capitulation, with Nebuchadnezzar putting his own puppet king on the throne, but the evidence is shaky either way. What we don't see as a result of Babylon's siege is the complete destruction of Tyre. This is where the "many nations" in Ezekiel 26:3 comes in. Tyre was never the same after the siege. It still had commercial strength, but nothing like it once had. Before, it possessed the economic power to take advantage of the nations, but now the nations turned that around by taking advantage of the struggling city. Even when the mainland city was rebuilt, it was nothing like its former glory.

Finally, in 332 BC, Alexander the Great came riding in with his unstoppable army. He demanded Tyre submit to him. The Tyrians said, "No." Alexander replied, "I was kinda hoping you'd say that." And he leveled the mainland part of the city. Out on the island, the city leaders were probably smugly saying, "Yeah, we've seen this before. They'll never reach us." But then they saw Alexander's army throwing rocks and debris into the water, and they said, "Uh-oh." Soon, a road was built through the water reaching all the way to the island. Alexander's army marched in, and that was it for Tyre. The mainland city would eventually be rebuilt, but without its former wealth or distinction or its island. This includes up to today. Tyre, Lebanon, is simply a medium-sized coastal city in a barely functioning nation.

A Song for Tyre (26–27)

Ezekiel now begins a series of four songs of lament. Two are for the city of Tyre, one for its prince, and one for its king. The first funeral song is in chapter 26 and simply communicates what the nations will sing about Tyre's fall. It is brief and it expresses the shock all will feel at the collapse of the once-great city.

The next three are more extensive, and their Writer was also the Author of Tyre's fate. Ezekiel was told by God to "take up a lamentation for Tyre" (27:2). When the prophet was ready with pen in hand, the Lord sang this dirge.

> O Tyre, you have said,
> "I am perfect in beauty."
> Your borders are in the midst of the seas.
> Your builders have perfected your beauty.
> They made all your planks of fir trees from Senir;
> they took a cedar from Lebanon to make you a mast.
> Of oaks from Bashan they made your oars;
> the company of Ashurites have inlaid your planks
> with ivory from the coasts of Cyprus.
> Fine embroidered linen from Egypt was what
>   you spread for your sail;
> blue and purple from the coasts of Elishah was
>   what covered you (verses 3-7).

Verse after verse, this song extolled the beauty and glory of the coastal kingdom. Then came the "but":

> But you are broken by the seas in the depths of
>   the waters;
> your merchandise and the entire company will fall
>   in your midst.
> All the inhabitants of the isles will be astonished at you;
> their kings will be greatly afraid,
> and their countenance will be troubled.
> The merchants among the peoples will hiss at you;
> you will become a horror, and be no more forever
> (verses 34–36).

In Scripture, when you see "but," it usually means everything is about to change. Sometimes it is for the good. "For the wages of sin is death, but the gift of God is eternal life in Christ Jesus our Lord" (Romans 6:23). You sin, you have earned yourself a death sentence. But eternal life is offered to you instead of eternal death. And, best yet, it's a free gift of God!

Tyre's lament had a different kind of "but." All was perfect. The people were on top of the world. But power, prestige, and wealth are fleeting. One moment, they were "perfect in beauty." The next, they were "a horror, and [will] be no more forever."

Two Songs for the Rulers of Tyre (28)

The first ruler lament is addressed to the *nagid* of Tyre. That Hebrew word is interesting because it means "ruler." Most versions translate it as "prince" to distinguish it from the man who will later be addressed in verse 11. The ruler of Tyre at the time of this prophecy was Ithobaal III, who apparently was pretty impressed with himself. This king reveled in his power and his wisdom. God, however, was having none of it. "You are a man, and not a god, though you set your heart as the heart of a god," the Lord told him, before adding parenthetically and quite sarcastically, "Behold, you are wiser than Daniel! There is no secret that can be hidden from you!" (28:2-3).

I love that the reputation of the wisdom of Daniel, an exiled eunuch Hebrew in the court of Nebuchadnezzar, was widespread enough that a pagan king in Tyre, around 1,000 kilometers or 600-plus miles away, knew he was getting slammed by God invoking the prophet's name. "You think you're smart, but are you Daniel-smart?"

Ithobaal III could make all the godhood claims he wanted, but there was one sure way to discover whether he was really a god. Just like when Jesus said that "wisdom is justified by her deeds" (Matthew 11:19 ESV), a king's deity is proven when his divine qualities are tested. According to the Lord, Ithobaal's would be tested, and they would fail.

> Will you still say before him who slays you, "I am a god"?
> But you shall be a man, and not a god, in the hand of
> him who slays you (Ezekiel 28:9).

As Lord Acton said, "Power tends to corrupt and absolute power corrupts absolutely."[5] Ithobaal was one more man who let his sycophants convince him that he was a god, until his enemies proved he was just another mortal man.

The second ruler lament is more interesting. Unlike the previous song, which was addressed to the *nagid*, or "ruler," this song is sung to the *melek*, or "king." *Melek* is a term that Ezekiel uses sparingly, and as we listen to this lament it becomes clear that, unless this passage is just a bunch of allegorical mush, the Lord isn't singing to any ordinary man. Or, more likely, not even to a man at all.

> Thus says the Lord GOD:
> "You were the seal of perfection,
>   full of wisdom and perfect in beauty.
> You were in Eden, the garden of God;
>   every precious stone was your covering…
> You were the anointed cherub who covers;
> I established you;
>   you were on the holy mountain of God;
>   you walked back and forth in the midst of fiery stones.
> You were perfect in your ways from the day you were created,
>   till iniquity was found in you" (verses 12-15).

Unlike the disdainful sarcasm directed at the prince of Tyre, there is genuine appreciation in the words we read here. The Creator is extolling the exquisite flawlessness of His creation. The recipient of these words is supernaturally outside of time, allowing him to have been active in the Garden of Eden as well as in Tyre. He is an angelic being, having been identified as a cherub. He carried out heavenly duties on the mountain of God. He was a joy to the Lord's heart. Till.

In the same way that "but" is a biblical turnaround word, so is "till." Everything was great till there was sin. And that sin changed everything. Instead of loyal service, there was animosity. Instead of fellowship, there was banishment. The Lord said, "Your heart was lifted up because of your beauty; you corrupted your wisdom for the sake of your splendor; I cast you to the ground, I laid you before kings, that they might gaze at you" (verse 17).

Who is this perfectly imperfect cherub? Some say he is the ideal man. Others that he is a false god. However, I'm thinking that you and I are on the same wavelength as Dr. Charles Dyer, who wrote:

> The best explanation is that Ezekiel was describing Satan who was the true "king" of Tyre, the one motivating the human "ruler" of Tyre. Satan was in the Garden of Eden (Gen. 3:1-7), and his chief sin was pride (1 Tim. 3:6). He also had access to God's presence (cf. Job 1:6-12). Speaking of God's judging the human "ruler" of Tyre for his pride (Ezek. 28:1-10), the prophet lamented the satanic "king" of Tyre who was also judged for his pride (vv. 11-19). Tyre was motivated by the same sin as Satan, and would suffer the same fate.[6]

Can I be dogmatic about my belief that this gives us insight into the transition of the anointed cherub Lucifer to the fallen angel Satan? I can't. But I'd put this one at about an eight out of ten. "But, Amir, what about the 'abundance of your trading' and the 'defiled...sanctuaries' and other stuff that doesn't really fit the devil?" You're exactly right—there are some things that don't fit. That is why I see this passage as a both/and. There were qualities of the king of Tyre's character and his living situation that were Luciferic enough for the Lord to use him as a teaching tool. It's like what we find with Antiochus IV and the antichrist in Daniel 11:21-35. We don't go in with the expectation that the actions of both will be exactly alike. Instead, we say, "Similar to Antiochus, the antichrist will…" In Ezekiel 28, we can ask, "Do you see how the king of Tyre had an extremely bloated view of his importance? It was pretty much like that before Satan's great fall." Numerous other similarities exist.

By the way, speaking of the antichrist, Ezekiel 28 has nothing to do with that future tribulational leader. Still, I regularly receive questions asking if this "anointed cherub" refers to him. Trust me, there are enough other passages in Scripture that give us insight into the character of the antichrist and his activities without having to shove his square peg into this round hole.

Wrapping It Up (28)

The chapter ends with a proclamation against Sidon and for Israel. Sidon was about 20 miles north of Tyre, along the Mediterranean coast, and, as a certain movie character would put it, "They got along like peas and carrots." The sins of Sidon were similar to those of Tyre, so rather than restating them all, they got the prophetic version of "ditto." God said, "I am against you…I will send pestilence…Then they shall know that I am the Lord" (verses 22-23).

As we've seen happen before, Ezekiel ends this tragic string of prophecies with a happy face for the future of Israel. Not only is the Lord bringing the people back from where they have been exiled, but once there, they will live safely and securely. This is because all the people who mocked them and hated on them will have been dealt with. God will be recognized for who He is. The Sidonians will understand Him through their destruction. And Israel will be drawn into fellowship with God through His incredible blessing.

CHAPTER 8

WITH FRENEMIES LIKE THESE

EZEKIEL 29-32

"A riddle wrapped in a mystery inside an enigma."[7] So went the great British Prime Minister Winston Churchill's description of the Soviet Union in October 1939. One year earlier, the German army had absorbed Austria in the Anschluss. European and American politicians were divided between appeasing the Third Reich and standing up against it.

Hitler was dangerous. Everyone, with the exception of the UK's Prime Minister Neville Chamberlain, could see it. Even the Soviet General Secretary Joseph Stalin wasn't a fan. Germany's strength was growing, and no one nation had the power to stand up against it.

Talks began that had the potential to forge a strong alliance between Western Europe and Russia. Only together could they stop the Nazi steamroller.

But then, out of the blue, Russia and Germany signed the Molotov-Ribbentrop Pact, creating an alliance between the two empires. The West was left wondering what the heck had just happened. One week later, Germany invaded Poland from the west, while Russia crossed the border from the east. Exactly one month after, Churchill made that famous statement about the incomprehensibility of the Russian mind.

To Churchill, who at the time was the First Lord of the Admiralty, the move by the Soviets made no long-term sense. Neither side could trust the other. But Stalin saw a cushion from the west in Poland and figured there was no way Hitler would be stupid enough to invade Russia and create a two-front war. Turns out *der Führer* was stupid enough after all, and that stupidity is what ultimately led to the fall of the Third Reich.

Why the history lesson? Because often, Russia and the West have found themselves in that awkward position of being frenemies. There have been times when the Kremlin and the capitals of Western Europe and America outright hated each other. I know many older folks from the West who remember drills that had them hiding under their desks at school in case Russia launched a nuclear attack. I must admit, though, that I'm not sure how the shelter of a desk would protect a child against a nuclear holocaust.

Other times, cooperation and even friendship have blossomed. As I was wrapping up the writing of this book, I watched as American astronauts Nick Hague, Suni Williams, and Butch Wilmore splashed down in the Atlantic Ocean off Tallahassee, Florida. But also returning from NASA's International Space Station in the SpaceX Dragon spacecraft was Russian cosmonaut Aleksandr Gorbunov. Best I could tell, everyone got along. The Russian wasn't shunned or made to sit with the luggage in the back of the spacecraft. Instead, there were hugs and smiles all around. All of this was taking place while President Donald Trump and President Vladimir Putin were in tense talks about the future of the Russia-Ukraine War. That is a frenemy.

That word also describes Israel's long-term relationship with Egypt. There were times from the very beginning when they got along. Sometime after Abram had brought his household into what would become the Promised Land, famine set in and "Abram went down to Egypt to dwell there, for the famine was severe in the land" (Genesis 12:10). Once there, he was welcomed by Pharaoh and allowed to live safely. All went well until the Egyptian ruler discovered that the woman Abram had called his sister was actually his wife. Pharaoh didn't find out about the ruse until after a pre-Mosaic series of plagues hit the ruler's house. Soon, the situation was remedied, and Pharaoh sent Abram away as quickly as possible. That is the very picture of a frenemy.

This not-quite-friend, oftentimes enemy relationship between Egypt and Israel continued through the years. To the Stockholm-syndromed minds of many of Moses' wilderness wanderers, it was worth a few blows from the truncheons of their former Egyptian buddies if it meant getting some of "the cucumbers, the melons, the leeks, the onions, and the garlic" (Numbers 11:4-5). Later in Israel's kingdom period, King Hoshea, the final monarch of the northern kingdom of Israel, became a vassal to Shalmaneser, king of Assyria. Hoshea reached out to Pharaoh to try to rekindle that frenemy relationship, hoping that Egypt would join forces with him and drive Assyria away. His plan didn't quite work out.

> The king of Assyria uncovered a conspiracy by Hoshea; for he had sent messengers to So, king of Egypt, and brought no tribute to the king of Assyria, as he had done year by year. Therefore the king of Assyria shut him up, and bound him in prison (2 Kings 17:4).

Something near 130 years later, King Zedekiah had the same idea. "Nebuchadnezzar expects me to pay him tribute? Nah, I'm done with that. I'm going to hit up my buddy down in Egypt, and together we're going to tell Babylon that it has no business on this side of the Fertile Crescent." As high as Zedekiah's opinion was of

Pharaoh Hophra, the Egyptian monarch's view of himself was even higher. Hophra even took credit for the creation of the Nile, saying, "My River is my own; I have made it for myself" (Ezekiel 29:3). As it turned out, neither estimation was justified. Ultimately, Nebuchadnezzar crushed both kingdoms under his feet.

Because of the close connection between Israel and Egypt over the course of many centuries, God took extra time with Ezekiel laying out the pharaonic kingdom's coming judgment. In the next several chapters, we have no less than seven messages the prophet was given to communicate to the once-great but now doomed Egyptian Empire.

Message #1–I Am Against You (29:1-17)

Ezekiel began this prophecy with a time stamp. In fact, six of the seven prophecies against Egypt began this way. The fall of a dynasty that was ancient even in sixth century BC was a momentous occurrence. The prophet was writing in a time when empires came and went. The Assyrians had been around for many years, but their militaristic expansion phase lasted about 300. Babylon, too, had been around for more than a millennia, but its great empire lasted less than 100. But the Egyptian dynasties had surfaced before 3000 BC. When the seemingly immortal civilization came crashing down, God wanted the world to know that it hadn't died of old age or poor management. The husk of the once-great power would be proof "that I am the Lord" (verse 6).

Ezekiel began "in the tenth year, in the tenth month, on the twelfth day of the month" (verse 1), or January 7, 587 BC. The beginning of the siege of Jerusalem was still a year off. The Lord called out Pharaoh and his arrogance, beginning with a devastating pronouncement. "Behold, I am against you, O Pharaoh king of Egypt" (verse 3). Can there be a more helpless position than to know that the almighty God of creation is against you? How do you defend yourself? Where can you possibly go to hide from His hand?

Crocodiles are terrifying animals. That seemingly lazy, docile creature can reach a speed of 11 miles per hour on land, and nearly 20 in the water. And if they catch you and get you in their jaws, expect to lose a limb, or more likely, your life.

Because crocodiles possess that much power, it is fascinating to watch a crocodile wrangler jump on the back of a beast, clamp its mouth shut with just his hands, then hold the giant maw closed with only a few layers of tape. The strength disparity between the closing muscles and the opening muscles of the crocodile jaw is so great that a mouth that can pulverize bone as it shuts can also be held tight by the human hand. This is the picture that God gave to Pharaoh. Calling Hophra the "great monster who lies in the midst of his rivers" (verse 3), the Lord said:

> I will put hooks in your jaws, and cause the fish of your rivers to stick to your scales; I will bring you up out of the midst of your rivers, and all the fish in your rivers will stick to your scales. I will leave you in the wilderness, you and all the fish of your rivers; you shall fall on the open field; you shall not be picked up or gathered (verses 4-5).

Mighty, like the crocodiles who ruled the waters of the Nile, Hophra believed he was an all-powerful god in his time. But crocs can be hunted and killed, and that was what the Lord had in mind for Pharaoh. Not only would the beast be dragged from the waters, but the fish that nourished the people would be stuck to him and pulled out too. Then, as the semiaquatic reptile slowly baked in the hot sun surrounded by flopping, dying fish, birds and other scavengers would come and eat away at him bite by bite. Not a pretty scene.

Not only would this be a message to the people of Egypt who were confronted with the realization that their Pharaoh-god was really just a mortal human, but it would also be a testament to all the other nations, including Israel and Judah, that Egypt could not be relied upon. The Assyrian envoys tried to convince King Hezekiah of that truth a century earlier when they said, "Look! You are trusting in the staff of this broken reed, Egypt, on which if a man leans, it will go into his hand and pierce it. So is Pharaoh king of Egypt to all who trust in him" (Isaiah 36:6). Now the Lord said essentially that same thing:

> Then all the inhabitants of Egypt shall know that I am the LORD. "Because you have been a staff of reed to the house of Israel, when they grasped you with the hand, you broke and tore all their shoulders; and when they leaned on you, you broke and made all their loins to shake" (Ezekiel 29:6-7 ESV).

Because God's people trusted in this braggadocious Pharaoh, the nation would suffer. For 40 years after Nebuchadnezzar brought the hurt to Egypt, the Egyptians themselves would be scattered. The land would be desolate and the cities laid waste. Finally, when the Lord would allow the people back into their land, it would never be the same. The days of the great empire were over. Said the Lord, "I will bring back the captives of Egypt and cause them to return to the land of Pathros, to the land of their origin, and there they shall be a lowly kingdom. It shall be the lowliest of kingdoms; it shall never again exalt itself above the nations, for I will diminish them so that they will not rule over the nations anymore" (verses 14-15). Looking at Egypt today, it is hard to imagine it being the superpower it once was. That's purposeful. The Lord wanted to ensure that no one would ever again depend upon an arrogant Egypt for protection, and He accomplished His goal thoroughly.

Message #2—The Fall of Egypt (29:17-21)

Ezekiel's prophecies tend toward the chronological. But between the first and second messages is a nearly 17-year jump. "The twenty-seventh year, in the first month, on the first day of the month" (verse 17) takes us all the way to April 26, 571 BC. If you'll remember, when Nebuchadnezzar laid siege to Tyre, he spent 13 long years there and came out with "Incomplete" written across the top of his exam. Frustrated and needing a financial infusion after all he had just spent, he turned south toward Egypt.

> Thus says the Lord God: "Surely I will give the land of Egypt to Nebuchadnezzar king of Babylon; he shall take away her wealth, carry off her spoil, and remove her pillage; and that will be the wages for his army. I have given him the land of Egypt for his labor, because they worked for Me," says the Lord God (verses 19-20).

What a fascinating statement. Babylon would gain victory over Egypt. How? God would give it to them. Why would He do that? Because Babylon had been a party in His overall plan. This is such a bizarre concept to contemplate using our kinder, gentler modern minds. Essentially, God was planning to reward the nation that wiped out His people, the Israelites, and His city, Jerusalem, for the very reason that they had just wiped out His people and His city. Nebuchadnezzar began with Israel, then he laid waste to a bunch of others too. These others deserved their destruction because they had cheered the Babylonians for doing the very thing God was now rewarding them for—that is, wiping out God's people, Israel. It's dizzying! And it gets even more crazy when we remember that the Lord then punished Babylon for its destruction of Jerusalem!

Is God fickle? Can He not make up His mind? In answer to the first question—no, and to the second—yes, He can. The almighty Nebuchadnezzar was an unknowing pawn in God's larger game. The Lord had plans for Israel, and a necessary step to carrying them out was destroying Jerusalem and clearing out most of the people. The king and his Babylonian horde were a bunch of killers looking for countries to invade and people to butcher, and Israel was on their hit list. God simply allowed them to do what they were determined to do. After Jerusalem, He allowed Nebuchadnezzar north toward Tyre, and the king went. While Babylon wasn't doing it for God, the Lord was still the beneficiary. So He let Nebuchadnezzar and his empire enjoy their wealth for a while, until it was time for them to face the wages of their brutal sins.

Could God have stopped Babylon from destroying Israel? Of course! Nothing could have been easier. But it isn't always the easy path that gets the necessary task accomplished. It's like when Jesus prayed in Gethsemane, "Father, if it is Your will, take this cup away from Me; nevertheless not My will, but Yours, be done" (Luke 22:42). The Son understood that there is sometimes a difficult price to pay for the Father's overall plan to be accomplished, and He was willing to pay that price. In Ezekiel's day, a purification of Israel was necessary. It was painful for the Lord to allow and heartbreaking for Him to watch, but it had to take place to move His people to the next stage in their eventual reconciliation with Him.

If God rewarded violent pagans like Nebuchadnezzar and his army for unknowingly accomplishing His will, how much more do you think He cherishes rewarding those of us who know Him and love Him and willingly serve Him? God is not like the miserly Ebenezer Scrooge, counting His thousand hills worth of cattle from a desk in a dark, underheated office, while one of his angels sits nearby tallying figures in the ledger and blowing on his tiny cherubic fingers trying to keep warm. No, our God is the Christmas-morning Scrooge whose greatest joy is giving gifts to others and bringing smiles to the faces of everyone He meets. Every time you serve Him, He sees. He's keeping His ledgers, and you are guaranteed to be rewarded.

Message #3—Egypt and the Nations (30:1-19)

The next prophecy is the only one in the series that is not dated. But we can infer by its subject matter that it came at the same time as the 587–585 BC messages. In this declaration, God had a word for Egypt and all its neighbors. Through Ezekiel, God said:

> The sword shall come upon Egypt, and great anguish shall be in Ethiopia, when the slain fall in Egypt, and they take away her wealth, and her foundations are broken down. Ethiopia, Libya, Lydia, all the mingled people, Chub, and the men of the lands who are allied, shall fall with them by the sword (30:4-5).

Principally, the Lord was saying that Nebuchadnezzar was going to sweep through northeastern Africa. Egypt at the top right of the continent, Libya to its left, Ethiopia down below, at least generally speaking. The borders were different then than they are now, but it is still all the same region. As always, God's purpose was the same as when He destroyed Egypt and her allies. "Then they will know that I am the Lord, when I have set a fire in Egypt and all her helpers are destroyed" (verse 8). God was showing Israel and the nations who He is.

Message #4—Broken-Armed Sword Play (30:20-26)

Now God's attention focused specifically on the arrogant, supposed river-making-god-man Pharaoh. The date was April 29, 587 BC, the year before Judah's fall to Nebuchadnezzar. The Lord knew that the people of Jerusalem were crying out to Egypt for help, and this was so frustrating for Him to watch. Why were they turning to a defeated king instead of the King of kings? Especially when it was the King of kings who ultimately was responsible for the defeat of the Egyptian king.

Son of man, I have broken the arm of Pharaoh king of Egypt; and see, it has not been bandaged for healing, nor a splint put on to bind it, to make it strong enough to hold a sword (verse 21).

Many believe this arm-breaking by God referred to the Lord handicapping Pharaoh's attempt to help Judah, thereby making Egypt useless. However, I think it is likely that this could be pointing all the way back to the Battle of Carchemish in 605 BC, when Egypt and Assyria were trounced by then-prince Nebuchadnezzar. While Assyria was decimated, Egypt slunk back home to lick its wounds and try to recover. However, it never could. Through Babylon, God had broken the arm of Pharaoh, and it would never reset properly.

"But, Amir, the Pharaoh at Carchemish was Necho II, but when Ezekiel prophesied this passage, the Pharaoh was Hophra." You are correct, and let me compliment you on your knowledge of Egyptian history. What God is saying is not just against a single Pharaoh, it's against the long line of Pharaohs that go back to the time when His people were slaves in Egypt. All these leaders believed they were gods, creators of the mighty Nile, first among all earthly rulers. God was about to show the world that a dying Pharaoh was no different than any other dying man.

> Thus says the Lord GOD: "Surely I am against Pharaoh king of Egypt, and will break his arms, both the strong one and the one that was broken; and I will make the sword fall out of his hand. I will scatter the Egyptians among the nations, and disperse them throughout the countries. I will strengthen the arms of the king of Babylon and put My sword in his hand; but I will break Pharaoh's arms, and he will groan before him with the groanings of a mortally wounded man" (verses 22-24).

What a picture! Pharaoh and Nebuchadnezzar are walking out on the battlefield to go *mano a mano* in a sword fight. Pharaoh shuffles out, the tip of his blade dragging in the dirt while the hand of his one good arm grasps tightly to the hilt. Meanwhile, the Babylonian king confidently struts out, his armor clanking against his powerfully built body with every step. His sword is gleaming in the sun, and his arms have been supernaturally strengthened by the Lord. As they draw closer, Pharaoh cries out and his sword drops to the ground. His one good arm is now cocked awkwardly with the bend of his arm not being located in a normal arm-bending place. There is no pity in Nebuchadnezzar's eyes. He only sees easy prey. Pharaoh drops to his knees and pitifully pleads for his life until Nebuchadnezzar's blade proves the Egyptian king's mortality.

With the death of Pharaoh will come a rout of the Egyptians. God described His actions and their reason, saying, "I will scatter the Egyptians among the nations and disperse them throughout the countries. Then they shall know that I am the Lord" (verse 26).

Message #5—Story Time for Pharaoh (31)

Another message, another time stamp. This one dated June 21, 587 BC. The beginning of this prophecy gives me the picture of the Lord telling Ezekiel to gather Pharaoh and his people around. Then, with a smile on his face, Ezekiel would say to them:

> Whom are you like in your greatness?
> Indeed Assyria *was* a cedar in Lebanon,
> with fine branches that shaded the forest,
> and of high stature;
> and its top was among the thick boughs.
> The waters made it grow;
> underground waters gave it height,
> with their rivers running around the place where it

> was planted,
> and sent out rivulets to all the trees of the field (31:2-4).

Everyone would have been enjoying the vibe of story time. There are far worse things to be compared to than the beauty and majesty of the Assyrian Empire in its heyday. The Lord continued to extol the great tree—its branches were long, its roots were deep. In fact, it was so beautiful that "all the trees of Eden envied it, that were in the garden of God" (verse 9).

Then in verse 10 came another of those words like "but" and "till." This one is "therefore," and whenever you see one of those, you have to ask, "What is it there for?" Here, it is a "because of" word. "Because of what you just read, therefore, this…" God said of Assyria that because it was so beautiful, its "heart was lifted up in its height" (verse 10). In other words, Assyria was beautiful, knew it was beautiful, and took full credit for its beauty.

That led to one more "therefore." Because of Assyria's pride in its majesty, "therefore I will deliver it into the hand of the mighty one of the nations, and he shall surely deal with it; I have driven it out for its wickedness" (verse 11). Through Ezekiel, God then described in detail the way that He brought down Assyria. At the end, He reminded His listeners, "This is Pharaoh and all his multitude" (verse 18).

The story had a little bit of a Nathan and David feel to it. After David took Bathsheba as his own and had her husband killed, the prophet Nathan confronted the king. He told the story of a rich man callously taking the only little companion lamb of a poor man, cooking it up, and serving it for dinner. David was enraged and swore vengeance on the rich man, to which Nathan replied, "You are the man!" (2 Samuel 12:7).

David's pride had swelled because he pictured himself as the great king who would right the wrong and make the man pay for his injustice. Then, in the blink of an eye, he realized that he was the man who deserved to be sanctioned. Similarly, Egypt's pride swelled as it was compared to the mighty Assyrians, until God quickly turned it around and said, "What I did to them, I'm going to do to you, also."

In life, there will be times of success. It may be in the family, at work, in the church, or any other situation, and accolades may come. But we can never forget who has given us our gifts, who has placed us in our positions, who has brought us friends and families and coworkers. With each accomplishment and every achievement, our first response must be to acknowledge the God responsible for it all, giving Him praise and honor for all we do.

Messages #6 and #7–The End of Egypt (32)

Two more messages; two more time stamps—March 3, 585 BC and April 1, 585 BC. Here we find the final nails in Egypt's coffin. In the first message, Ezekiel was instructed to sing a lamentation over the death of the once-great empire. "When I put out your light, I will cover the heavens, and make its stars dark; I will cover the sun with a cloud, and the moon shall not give her light…When I make the land of Egypt desolate, and the country is destitute of all that once filled it, then I strike all who dwell in it, then they shall know that I am the Lord" (32:7, 15). When God brings His judgment, there is no gloating. Once again, a civilization that had the potential to be great if it had followed Him became crass, disgusting, and worthless because it chose to follow other gods.

In the final message, Ezekiel was not told to sing a sad song, but rather, to "wail over the multitude of Egypt" (verse 18). They were headed to where everyone goes who does not know the Lord. It doesn't matter what you were in life; in death, everyone apart from the Lord is the same. Down in the depths of the earth was Assyria and Elam, both with their multitudes and all their dead. Meshech and Tubal were there, along with Edom and the Sidonians. All of them were "slain by the sword" and all conscripted "to the Pit" (verse 29).

King Solomon wrote, "Do not rejoice when your enemy falls, and do not let your heart be glad when he stumbles; lest the Lord see it, and it displease Him, and He turn away His wrath from him" (Proverbs 24:17). This is why Ezekiel is told to wail and not to rejoice.

I live in a nation surrounded by threats. And I celebrate when a threat is ended. I can be satisfied that the person will face both temporal and eternal justice. However, I know that we must never gloat over a fallen enemy. Love your enemies. Pray for those who persecute you. That is the calling given to all believers in Yeshua—even to those living with Hamas right on the other side of the border.

CHAPTER 9

THE TURNING OF THE PAGE

EZEKIEL 33–35

Years back, I can remember walking through a Sharper Image store while on a speaking tour. At that time, Sharper Image was a place in which one could find cool, unexpected products like lighted balls that create a starscape on a ceiling and small guns to rapidly inflate tires and reusable glowing ice cubes in festive shapes. Of course, if one was available, you couldn't miss some relaxation time in their magnificent massage chairs that would provide you with five or ten minutes of full shiatsu bliss.

During that particular visit, I found myself in a section dedicated to desk décor. Littering the shelves were small gadgets and puzzles designed to delight office visitors or to provide your hands with something to do during long conference calls. One item in particular caught my interest. Inside a glowing crescent, a globe floated. No wires, no strings, no little streams of air blowing on the top and bottom. The world just hung there like magic. Gently, I spun the ball, and it twirled in place. I twisted it back the other way, and still it remained. Then I gave it a little tap on the bottom, and it shot up to the top of the crescent. That's when it all made sense. Magnets! The manufacturer of this slick little device had used magnetic levitation to create a system that utilized the repelling nature of like poles. It was brilliant. Not brilliant enough for me to shell out the shekels to buy it, but still brilliant.

It's amazing what a little information can do. What could have been chalked up to electrical current or air flow or magic or witchcraft all boiled down to a simple magnetic principle. A similarly small amount of information is all we need to understand the final destruction of Jerusalem too. There are many in-depth explanations we can postulate as to why Israel fell—some historical, some geopolitical, some religious, some ethnic. The true answer, however, is much simpler, and when you understand it, everything makes sense.

Jerusalem's demise all comes down to the covenants—the deals that God made with His people. It is in these promises that the onus for Jerusalem's destruction is removed from God's seemingly vindictive shoulders and placed squarely on the willful rebellion of the people. It is also there where we are blessedly reminded that what is taking place is not a full stop in the relationship between God and His chosen people, but just a significant bump in the road.

In Ezekiel 33–35, we enter a transition point in the prophet's book and in the history of Israel. The destruction of the past is wrapping up and the hope of the nation's future is about to be revealed. But before we go there, we should ground ourselves again. We need a reminder of the four covenants—three unconditional and one conditional—that provide the foundation for the relationship between God and Israel.

The Abrahamic Covenant

God established an unconditional promise with Abraham that launched the relationship between Him and His people.

> I will make you a great nation; I will bless you and make your name great; and you shall be a blessing. I will bless

those who bless you, and I will curse him who curses you; and in you all the families of the earth shall be blessed (Genesis 12:2-3).

In this and several other iterations given throughout Abraham's lifetime, the Lord promised the patriarch people, land, and blessing. Has He kept His promise? I am living proof that Abraham's people still exist. The country in which I live is affirmation that the land still belongs to Abraham's descendants. And you can ask the Assyrians, the Babylonians, the Romans, and the Third Reich, amongst many others, whether God blesses those who bless Israel and curses those who curse Israel. Come to think of it, you can't ask them. They're all gone, but somehow Israel still survives.

The destruction of Judah was a glitch in the relationship between God and Israel. True, it was a serious glitch, but it was not the deal-breaker that some claim it is. The contract itself cannot be broken because there was no obedience clause included in Abraham's part of the covenant. God said, "I will," and never integrated an addendum that began, "And I expect you to…" Israel was God's chosen people, is God's chosen people, and always will be God's chosen people.

The Mosaic Covenant

The second covenant came with Moses, and, unlike any of the others, it was conditional. It is extremely important that we always keep this distinction in mind. There is nothing in this transaction made with Moses that will or can affect God's word to the patriarchs. With the other covenants, it was purely promises made, promises kept. That is the nature of our God.

The Mosaic covenant, however, was based on "If you do this, then I will do that." To this covenant, God attached the promise of wonderful blessing. But to receive it, the people of Israel would have to abide by a code of rules. If the nation chose not to follow those rules, a harsh set of consequences would result. Avoiding the choice wasn't an option. It was purely either/or.

"But how is that fair, Amir? God forced a covenant on the people and told them that they had better obey Him or else!" If that was how the transaction went down, then I might agree with you. But this covenant wasn't forced on anyone. It was offered, and the people willfully accepted it.

> Then [Moses] took the Book of the Covenant and read in the hearing of the people. And they said, "All that the LORD has said we will do, and be obedient." And Moses took the blood, sprinkled it on the people, and said, "This is the blood of the covenant which the LORD has made with you according to all these words" (Exodus 24:7-8).

An amazing time of fellowship between God and man immediately followed this affirmation of the covenant, during which Moses, Aaron, two of Aaron's sons, and 70 elders of Israel "saw the God of Israel" (verses 9-10). So much hope; so much potential. Then came the golden calf, the grumbling and rebellion, the period of the judges, all the bad kings, and the immoral depths of idolatry.

What began as an unparalleled moment during which 74 Hebrews witnessed the throne room of God all at one time deteriorated to the point of Babylon laying siege to Jerusalem. It was all because one party failed to remain true to this mutual promise. Israel abandoned the covenant, but God didn't. Therefore, the responsibility for Jerusalem's destruction and the killing of so many people lay solely in the nation's unfaithfulness.

The Davidic Covenant

There are still two more covenants. Both are unconditional, and both are spectacular. The first was given to King David through the prophet Nathan:

> When your days are fulfilled and you rest with your fathers, I will set up your seed after you, who will come from your body, and I will establish his kingdom. He shall build a house for My name, and I will establish the throne of his kingdom forever. I will be his Father, and he shall be My son. If he commits iniquity, I will chasten him with the rod of men and with the blows of the sons of men. But My mercy shall not depart from him, as I took it from Saul, whom I removed from before you. And your house and your kingdom shall be established forever before you. Your throne shall be established forever (2 Samuel 7:12-16).

Any sign of a "if you do this, I will do that" in this promise? Absolutely not. This is God saying, "I will," and asking nothing in return. Why would the Lord make this eternal promise to a man whose flaws became so public and brought about such wide-reaching consequences? Thousands died due to David's sins throughout his reign.

God knew who David was inside. He knew that although he had his failings, the king was a man after His own heart (1 Samuel 13:14; Acts 13:22). It was because of that deep dedication that God blessed David with this covenant despite his weaknesses.

We must never lose sight of how perfect the mercy and forgiveness of our God is. You may have actions in your past that have you wondering if God could ever forgive you and use you again. Or you may be in the midst of an ongoing sin right now, too caught up to stop and too embarrassed and ashamed to ask for help from God or a friend or pastor. Do not give up on yourself, because God has not given up on you. Remember, in Jerusalem, the glory of the Lord was still at the temple up until the end. All it would have taken for the people of Jerusalem to save themselves and their city was to turn back, confess, and worship the Lord. He was right there waiting for them. The Holy Spirit, God's glory in every believer, is still with you too. Let today be the day you return to Him and start anew. Then go to a pastor or close friend and let them begin walking with you on your journey back to the Lord.

The New Covenant

Some reading this book may be thinking, *Finally, we're getting to the church—the recipients of the new covenant!* If that's you, I'm afraid I have some bad news. Every one of these four covenants are for Israel, the people of the covenant.

Okay, I know I've stirred up a hornet's nest by saying that the new covenant is for Israel. So let me quickly ask the Lord to come to my aid:

> Behold, the days are coming, says the LORD, when I will make a new covenant with the house of Israel and with the house of Judah—not according to the covenant that I made with their fathers in the day that I took them by the hand to lead them out of the land of Egypt, My covenant which they broke, though I was a husband to them, says the LORD (Jeremiah 31:31-32).

Those are God's words, not mine! The new covenant is a Jewish covenant, made with the house of Israel and the house of Judah. It's true that Jesus is the mediator of the new covenant, and that many of the spiritual blessings of the covenant are received by the church. But its origins and foundation are with Israel. Undoubtedly, the Israelites failed badly, but man's failure in no way negates God's faithfulness.

> This is the covenant that I will make with the house of Israel after those days, says the LORD: I will put My law in their minds, and write it on their hearts; and I will be their God, and they shall be My people. No more shall

every man teach his neighbor, and every man his brother, saying, "Know the Lord," for they all shall know Me, from the least of them to the greatest of them, says the Lord. For I will forgive their iniquity, and their sin I will remember no more (verses 33-34).

So many have tried to manipulate this into a church-directed promise, but the Lord couldn't have been clearer about whom He was speaking to. It's "with the house of Israel." If anyone is still doubting, they need only to keep reading, because context is king!

> Thus says the Lord,
> who gives the sun for a light by day,
> the ordinances of the moon and the stars for a light by night,
> who disturbs the sea,
> and its waves roar
> (the Lord of hosts is His name):
>
> "If those ordinances depart
> from before Me, says the Lord,
> then the seed of Israel shall also cease
> from being a nation before Me forever."
>
> Thus says the Lord:
>
> "If heaven above can be measured,
> and the foundations of the earth searched out beneath,
> I will also cast off all the seed of Israel
> for all that they have done, says the Lord"
> (verses 35-37).

There is no allusion in those words to the church or a future nation—spiritual or otherwise. God said that He would make a new covenant with Israel, His people. Anyone who thinks He was done with them for good needs to think again. When the sun stops shining, the moon and the stars disappear, and the waves break over the shores and flood the land, then you can consider that maybe God is done with Israel. Or when you have an accurate measurement of the universe down to the millimeter and have mapped out every aspect of inner earth, then God will consider casting aside His people.

This unassailable faithfulness is true for anyone with whom God makes a commitment, and that should lift your spirits high if you are a believer in the Messiah. Once you belong to God, you always belong to God because He cares for each one of His children with the same love and grace that He has for the nation of Israel.

The End Is Coming (33:1-20)

Before we move on to new beginnings, we need to deal with final endings. Chapter 33 was God's final justification to Israel and the world that what was about to happen to Jerusalem was righteous and proper and should be a surprise to no one.

The people had been warned. God had sent Ezekiel as a watchman to tell the people that judgment was near. "You, son of man: I have made you a watchman for the house of Israel; therefore you shall hear a word from My mouth and warn them for Me" (33:7). From the beginning of Ezekiel's book, God placed the prophet on the wall to warn the Jerusalemites. But the people chose to ignore him. And not just him, but all the other watchmen whom God had sent.

> Thus says the LORD: "Stand in the ways and see, and ask for the old paths, where the good way is, and walk in it; then you will find rest for your souls. But they said, 'We will not walk in it.' Also, I set watchmen over you, saying, 'Listen to the sound of the trumpet!' But they said, 'We will not listen'" (Jeremiah 6:16-17).

The Lord twice pleaded for the people to change their ways. "Remember the old times when we were good together? Please go back to them and it will all be wonderful again." They said, "No."

"I've given you watchmen. Will you at least listen to them?" The people covered their ears with their hands and walked away, sealing their doom as the Babylonian army approached.

The words once again are so much like when Jesus mourned over Jerusalem, wishing He could have gathered the people like chicks. Here, God grieved over what was about to happen, pleading with the people to turn back to Him:

> "As I live," says the Lord GOD, "I have no pleasure in the death of the wicked, but that the wicked turn from his way and live. Turn, turn from your evil ways! For why should you die, O house of Israel?" (Ezekiel 33:11).

The destruction of Jerusalem was not a "want to" on God's part, but a "have to." Sin must be paid for. Again, the cries sounded out of "Unfair, God! You're being cruel! You're making us pay for the sins of others!" But He quickly shut them down. The people of Jerusalem were not paying for the sins of their ancestors or even of their fellow citizens. Their punishment came because of their own rejection of God and rebellion against His law. The Lord told the people, "You say, 'The way of the LORD is not fair.' O house of Israel, I will judge every one of you according to his own ways" (verse 20). All have sinned. All have fallen short of the glory of God. Now it was time for the people of Jerusalem to receive the wages of their sins.

The End Has Come (33:21-22)

The day was January 8, 585 BC. Ezekiel suspected that Jerusalem's time had passed. It was likely that his fellow countrymen had been slaughtered, the city destroyed, and, worst of all, the temple demolished. In his home where he always remained, he sat silently waiting for word from the city so far to the west.

The door burst open, and a man ran in. The visitor was dirt-caked and disheveled. His clothes were ragged, and his broken-down sandals barely clung to his feet. Before Ezekiel could welcome the man or invite him to sit down, the messenger blurted out, "The city has been captured!" (verse 21).

Tears flooded the prophet's eyes as he sighed and nodded his sorrow. He had expected to hear something like this today. The previous night, the Lord had visited him. The restrictions on his speech had been lifted, which indicated to the prophet that his era of being a watchman were at an end. There were no more chances for the once-great city; the opportunity for repentance was past. What was done was done. Jerusalem was no more.

Don't Think You've Gotten Away with Anything (33:23-33)

In one sense, the message may have been a relief for Ezekiel. Maybe he was done with prophesying. Suddenly, being a watchman now for the city of Jerusalem was like being a store manager for Blockbuster video. It was great to have the fancy title, but a watchman without a city was just a guy standing on a wall.

For Ezekiel, however, there was no release from the title *prophet*. Plenty of people still needed to hear the words of the Lord. There was the remnant back in Jerusalem. Many of them were considering their survival as some sort of sign that they were blessed by God. "Abraham was only one, and he inherited the land. But we are many; the land has been given to us as a possession" (verse 24), they said, claiming that their continued existence meant God was blessing them with the land. Sure, Jerusalem would need a little sprucing up; they would have to clear some rubble here and there. But because they were the favored survivors of the invasion, God would likely help with that too.

The Lord's answer to their delusional thinking would have sent shivers deep into their bones. They were just as bad of sinners as the ones who had died, God told them. And it was likely a day would come that they would wish they, too, had been slaughtered by the Babylonians. "Then they shall know that I am the Lord, when I have made the land most desolate because of all their abominations which they have committed" (verse 29).

But it wasn't just the people left in Jerusalem who still had a lesson to learn. It was Ezekiel's fellow exiles. It's interesting to note here how the prophet communicates his prophecies. I think when we picture the great prophets speaking forth God's words, we have in our minds something like Charlton Heston's Moses in *The Ten Commandments*, as he stands before the people with his booming voice and outstretched arms. But here we see a very different style of communication.

> They come to you as people do, they sit before you as My people, and they hear your words, but they do not do them; for with their mouth they show much love, but their hearts pursue their own gain. Indeed you are to them as a very lovely song of one who has a pleasant voice and can play well on an instrument; for they hear your words, but they do not do them (verses 31-32).

I will readily admit my bias, but I think biblical songs passionately sung in Hebrew to a very simple accompaniment is like the music of angels. Whether you understand the words or not, the emotion and reverence inherent in the praise grab your heart and lift it to heavenly realms.

God told Ezekiel that the people came to him simply for a heavenly worship fix.

"Hey, I hear that Ezekiel is playing down at the amphitheater by the River Chebar!"

"Sweet! I hope he does the 'Fall of Tyre' again. I love singing along with that one!"

This reminds me of the sin-on-Saturday and pray-on-Sunday church attenders. Talk to the pastor of any congregation; they know who they are. These men and women want to feel the emotion of worship, but they don't want the responsibility of obedience. They feel good because singing about God gives them the warmies inside, and the pastor's sermon is usually just long enough to get the after-church grocery shopping list written out. The Lord warned Ezekiel that this is who the people were. Nothing had changed since the exile. But one day they would find out that emotion is not enough for a relationship.

There's a New Shepherd in Town (34)

We have now reached a pivotal chapter in the book of Ezekiel. God had given incredible autonomy to the leaders of Israel to either follow Him or reject Him. Not only did they choose to reject Him, but they led all the people to rebel against God also. Like worthless hired shepherds, the religious and political hierarchy cared only about their own comfort and wealth.

> Thus says the Lord GOD to the shepherds: "Woe to the shepherds of Israel who feed themselves! Should not the shepherds feed the flocks? You eat the fat and clothe yourselves with the wool; you slaughter the fatlings, but you do not feed the flock...So they were scattered because there was no shepherd; and they became food for all the beasts of the field when they were scattered" (34:2-3, 5).

Not a great resumé, especially for someone responsible for taking care of the precious flock of God. The Lord's shepherds should have the kind of stellar CV that would have flock owners around the world pounding down the doors trying to hire them on. Instead, these herders were not only useless, but harmful. So God fired them. He said, "Behold, I am against the shepherds, and I will require My flock at their hand" (verse 10).

But what was to be done now with the leaderless sheep? Not only were they clueless about how to care for themselves, but all the habits they'd learned from the previous shepherds were bad. It would take wisdom, commitment, sacrifice, and time to get this flock back on the straight and narrow. Who was up to this challenge? "I am," said God.

> Thus says the Lord God: "Indeed I Myself will search for My sheep and seek them out. As a shepherd seeks out his flock on the day he is among his scattered sheep, so will I seek out My sheep and deliver them from all the places where they were scattered on a cloudy and dark day. And I will bring them out from the peoples and gather them from the countries, and will bring them to their own land; I will feed them on the mountains of Israel, in the valleys and in all the inhabited places of the country. I will feed them in good pasture, and their fold shall be on the high mountains of Israel. There they shall lie down in a good fold and feed in rich pasture on the mountains of Israel. I will feed My flock, and I will make them lie down," says the Lord God. "I will seek what was lost and bring back what was driven away, bind up the broken and strengthen what was sick; but I will destroy the fat and the strong, and feed them in judgment" (verses 11-16).

What an amazing passage! God had left it to the amateurs, and they had botched it up. Now He was stepping in and taking over. He had been without His people for too long, and it was time to start bringing them back to the pen. What we read in the rest of chapter

34 are four specific activities that the Shepherd would carry out. The timeframe for these great accomplishments would be threefold—Ezekiel's time, our time, and the future.

Activity #1—Gathering the Sheep Home

When the Assyrians conquered the northern kingdom of Israel, the Jewish people were scattered throughout the empire. With the Babylonian invasion, the people of the southern kingdom of Judah were exiled to Nebuchadnezzar's empire. Most of those left in Israel ignored God's command to stay put and trust His provision, choosing instead to flee down to Egypt, where they met their demise. Left in the land were small handfuls of people—the remnant—scattered, impoverished, pitiful. But with the new Shepherd in town, that was all about to change.

As we saw in the passage above, God went on a hunt for His sheep, tracking them down and bringing them home to their pen in Israel. First, with Zerubbabel, then with Ezra and Nehemiah and others. Over the years, the land began to repopulate. Its initial impetus was God softening the heart of King Cyrus, something that only the Great Shepherd could do.

This didn't happen only in Ezekiel's time, though. In the late nineteenth century, God began calling His people back home to Israel. They had been scattered all across the earth following the Roman diaspora in the first and second centuries AD. But God called out the names of His people, and, like sheep when they hear the voice of their Shepherd, multitudes of Jews from all over the world flocked home.

Activity #2—Feeding and Caring for the Sheep

When the people of Israel came home after the exile, most didn't do so empty-handed. They returned with what their families had been able to accumulate through 70 years of hard work and establishing a life in and around Babylon. That doesn't mean they were all prosperous. It was a difficult existence, but God carried them through. They had their stupid moments when the Shepherd had to take out His rod and discipline His problem sheep, like the usurers and those who took fellow Israelites as slaves. But over time, the land healed and the people healed, and Israel was once again comfortable and at peace, for the most part.

The same is true in today's latter return. What had become a malarial, barren nightmare of a land was revived and restored by the returning Jews. Now, Israel is the number one military power in the Middle East. Its farmlands are fertile and its people well-fed. The technology coming out of the "Silicone Wadi" rivals that of anywhere else in the world. In fact, the 2024 World Happiness Report ranked Israel eighth on its list![8] When the right Shepherd is in charge, it is amazing what can be done.

Activity #3—Setting Up Righteous Leaders

The pre-exilic batch of leaders was a worthless lot. "Behold, I shall judge between sheep and sheep, between rams and goats. Is it too little for you to have eaten up the good pasture, that you must tread down with your feet the residue of your pasture—and to have drunk of the clear waters, that you must foul the residue with your feet?" (verses 17-18). You just couldn't get good help in those days.

For the exilic returnees, the Lord took the lead, filtering out the bad leaders and replacing them with the good. As was evident, particularly in Nehemiah, there was no shortage of bad leaders still around. But in the future, God has something special planned. He's bringing in a ringer.

> I will establish one shepherd over them, and he shall feed them—My servant David. He shall feed them and be their shepherd. And I, the Lord, will be their God, and My

servant David a prince among them; I, the Lord, have spoken (verses 23-24).

Yes, that David! As the Lord rules over the earth from Jerusalem, a resurrected David will rule over the nation of Israel. If you think that sounds bizarre, just remember that if you know Jesus as your Lord and Savior, then the resurrected you will be there, too, witnessing the man after God's own heart sitting on the throne. That is a sight I cannot wait to see! We'll get into this more in the next chapter.

Activity #4—Reigning over the Millennium

Verses 25 through 30 give a beautiful picture of what the 1,000-year reign of Christ will be like. But it is only a taste. Much more on that is coming at the end of Ezekiel. We just know this era will be unlike anything we've experienced. A time with no devil and with our Lord ruling over us in bodily form. The final verse in the chapter perfectly expresses the feel of this unique time in history. "'You are My flock, the flock of My pasture; you are men, and I am your God,' says the Lord God" (verse 31). Love, loyalty, benevolence, subservience, peace, protection, provision, joy, satisfaction—the list of descriptors is endless. What a time it will be when we can worship our Messiah and Lord face to face!

From Seir to Eternity (35)

Ugh! The literary flow was so perfect. In chapter 33, we had the final condemnation and fall of Jerusalem. In chapter 34, God took over as Shepherd. In chapters 36 and 37, we have the restoration of the land and people in preparation for God leading the children of Israel to repentance. In chapters 38 and 39, we have the Ezekiel war, which will position Israel and the world for the coming of the antichrist and the tribulation. Then in chapter 40 and beyond, we witness a repentant Israel enjoying the 1,000-year rule of the Messiah on earth.

Then there's chapter 35 and its judgment on Mount Seir right in the middle of the flow. Why? It seems like this would have fit so much better back in chapter 25, when there was a whole list of nations being judged. And, in a sense, it had been included. Mount Seir is essentially Edom, its geographical area being that in which Edom was located.

Its name even fits the Edom motif. If you remember from earlier, *Edom* means "red." *Seir* means "hairy." A hairy red guy—that sounds a lot like Esau, who settled the region. In fact, when Jacob was returning home after his long sojourn up north, he was rightfully afraid of his brother's reaction to him being back in the neighborhood. As a heads up, Jacob "sent messengers before him to Esau his brother in the land of Seir, the country of Edom" (Genesis 32:3). So even while Jacob was tending sheep for Laban and fathering the 12 tribes of Israel, Esau was setting up shop down in Seir.

I've promised you that I will always let you know when I am speculating. What I am about to tell you makes sense to me biblically and logically, but I cannot 100 percent prove it. So, take this for what it's worth, and if you're reading this book as part of a Bible study, you can get together and tell each other why I'm wrong.

Isaac's wife, Rebekah, became pregnant and gave birth to twins. The older, as we've just mentioned, was red, hairy Esau. The younger was less-red, less-hairy Jacob. As the brothers grew up, Esau became an outdoorsman, while Jacob liked to hang around camp. At one point, Esau came to Jacob after a long hunt, famished and begging for some food. "Sell me your birthright as of this day," said Jacob (Genesis 25:31). Esau agreed.

Later, as Isaac was preparing to give his fatherly blessing to his older son Esau, Jacob, at Rebekah's insistence, deceived his father and took the blessing for himself. Dad was heartbroken, Esau was infuriated, Jacob was confused, and Rebekah smirked and thought, *Moms rule the family.* But as much as Rebekah believed she had manufactured this great family coup, it all was according to God's plan. The Lord had already made His choice as to who would carry the line of Abraham. That honor belonged to the younger Jacob, who would later bear the name Israel. As God said through Malachi, "Jacob I have loved; but Esau I have hated, and laid waste his mountains and his heritage for the jackals of the wilderness" (Malachi 1:2-3). Ezekiel 35 is a prophecy of the laying waste of Esau's mountains.

"But, Amir, how is that fair? Why would God take away Esau's right as firstborn?" Good question, and you're not the first to ask it. In fact, when Paul quoted those verses from Malachi, others wondered the same thing. The apostle responded very matter-of-factly:

> What shall we say then? Is there injustice on God's part? By no means! For he says to Moses, "I will have mercy on whom I have mercy, and I will have compassion on whom I have compassion." So then it depends not on human will or exertion, but on God, who has mercy (Romans 9:14-16 ESV).

Paul told the people, "At some point, you just have to trust God. This may not make sense to you, but it does to Him. So, you're either going to have faith that He will always act according to His perfect character or you're not."

God chose Jacob over Esau and Jacob's descendants over Esau's. In Ezekiel chapters 35 and 36, we see this choice played out in the prophecies of the mountains. To Esau's descendants, the Lord said through the prophet:

> Son of man, set your face against Mount Seir and prophesy against it, and say to it, "Thus says the Lord GOD: 'Behold, O Mount Seir, I am against you; I will stretch out My hand against you, and make you most desolate; I shall

lay your cities waste, and you shall be desolate. Then you shall know that I am the Lord'" (Ezekiel 35:2-4).

With their swords, the people of Mount Seir slaughtered the Israelites, and with their mouths, they mocked their suffering and agony. "As you rejoiced because the inheritance of the house of Israel was desolate, so I will do to you; you shall be desolate, O Mount Seir, as well as all of Edom—all of it! Then they shall know that I am the Lord" (verse 15).

Ezekiel is then told to "prophesy to the mountains of Israel" (36:1). But this message is very different. Instead of destruction and annihilation, Israel is promised life and restoration.

> You, O mountains of Israel, you shall shoot forth your branches and yield your fruit to My people Israel, for they are about to come. For indeed I am for you, and I will turn to you, and you shall be tilled and sown. I will multiply men upon you, all the house of Israel, all of it; and the cities shall be inhabited and the ruins rebuilt. I will multiply upon you man and beast; and they shall increase and bear young; I will make you inhabited as in former times, and do better for you than at your beginnings. Then you shall know that I am the Lord (verses 8-11).

What a contrast! What a testimony to God fulfilling His promises! Both Edom and Israel were idolatrous nations, rebellious against the true God and steeped in sin. But centuries earlier, God had made a choice between two brothers. To Jacob He had made a promise, saying,

> I am the Lord God of Abraham your father and the God of Isaac; the land on which you lie I will give to you and your descendants. Also your descendants shall be as

the dust of the earth; you shall spread abroad to the west and the east, to the north and the south; and in you and in your seed all the families of the earth shall be blessed (Genesis 28:13-14).

God's promises have been and will be fulfilled just as He said. Seir would be brought down for its sins, while God's chosen people continue their trajectory toward an eternal kingdom. Once all is fulfilled, then everyone will know that He is the Lord!

CHAPTER 10

REBIRTH

EZEKIEL 36-37

Believe it or not, I'm not a perfect man. I know, I know, some of you are reeling in shock right now. Those who actually know me, however, are saying, "Wow, Amir, why don't you drop another surprise truth on us, like the sky is blue or water is wet!"

It's true. There are times when I disappoint my family, my Behold Israel team, my friends, and, most importantly, my God. Sin is a sad part of this mortal life we are living. I long for the day when I will shed this corruptible shell for a new, upgraded incorruptible body.

For those times when I do fail, there is a passage written by Paul that always boosts me up and keeps me going. The apostle wrote, "One thing I do, forgetting those things which are behind and reaching forward to those things which are ahead, I press toward the goal for the prize of the upward call of God in Christ Jesus" (Philippians 3:13-14). Putting the past behind and setting your sights on the future—that is an essential philosophy for anyone who wants to serve God. Wallowing in our sins leads to inertia. We give in to the devil's lies of "You're not good enough," and "Who would ever listen to you now?" That kind of self-imposed guilt makes us useless in God's kingdom.

Spiritual shame is unwarranted and unnecessary for the believer in the Messiah. When we confess, God forgives. And when God forgives, He does so completely. If guilt short-circuits our service to God, it's not the Holy Spirit who is putting on the brakes. That is the enemy trying to take our legs out from under us before we have the chance to do some good for the kingdom.

With Jesus, when we "confess our sins, He is faithful and just to forgive us our sins and to cleanse us from all unrighteousness" (1 John 1:9). That doesn't mean that our forgiven sins are filed away in a cabinet for a future reckoning. God isn't keeping our offences in a computer folder, ready to download it into our brains the moment we start feeling confident about our Christian walk. When we confess, our sins are tossed into the incinerator, never to be seen again.

But there is a nuance to the phrase "forget our sins." The "forget" here has the sense of "not letting it negatively impact." It doesn't mean our sins never enter our minds again. We've got to learn from our mistakes. If I sin once, then I'm a sinner. If I commit that same sin again, then I'm a sinner and an idiot because I didn't learn the first time. We forget our sins to the extent that guilt doesn't oppress us and make us unusable. We remember our sins so that we don't fall into the same trap again.

As we approach Ezekiel 36 and 37, we are in the preparation stage for Israel to put the past behind and press on to the goal. God could have changed the hearts of the people in one quick Holy Spirit blast. Bam! Suddenly every Jew around the world is praising Yeshua as the Messiah. But God appreciates process, and His definition of love demands free will. He knows what it will take to bring His people to their knees, and He is committed to a worship that is birthed in a recognition of who He is, not from some divine mandate. In these two chapters of Ezekiel, we see God laying the tracks for the redemptive train that will carry Israel to a final and permanent reconciliation with Him.

Prophetic Fulfillments

Proclaiming prophecies is a risk. A prophet puts himself out on a limb by saying, "Just wait. This is going to happen." What if it doesn't? What does that say about the prophet and his foretelling skills? That's why I don't understand these online pastors who predict the day of the rapture using blood moons or festivals or political events or some secret code they found hidden within the ancient manuscripts. Inevitably, the fateful day will come, and they and their followers will prepare for flight. From morning to night, they sit excitedly anticipating that feeling of liftoff. But nothing happens—as always. The pastor disappears for a while, mumbling something about missing a digit or misreading some Aramaic inscription. But then, three months later, he's back with a new date, saying he figured out the problem from last time. And, for some reason, people still believe him! Oy vey, what a *balagan*!

But for God, prophecy is not a risk for two reasons. First, He has seen all history from beginning to end.

> Remember the former things of old, for I am God, and there is no other; I am God, and there is none like Me, declaring the end from the beginning, and from ancient times things that are not yet done, saying, "My counsel shall stand, and I will do all My pleasure" (Isaiah 46:9-10).

There is nothing that will happen on this earth that God does not intimately know about.

But it's more than Him simply witnessing it. He has ordained it. God's not sitting around gazing at the world's timeline, watching what we humans decide to do, jotting down notes on a yellow legal pad for future prophetic reference. He is the One who is in control. Of course, He gives us freedom, as long as that freedom stays within His overall will. But God will accomplish His purposes, and He will use nations and people to do it. So as we look at the prophecies that fill the remaining pages of Ezekiel's book, we can do so with the certainty that it is not *if* these things will happen, but *when*.

With prophecy, there are often two fulfillments—a near and a far. For instance, through Ezekiel, God promised a return from exile:

> "I will gather you from the peoples, assemble you from the countries where you have been scattered, and I will give you the land of Israel." And they will go there, and they will take away all its detestable things and all its abominations from there (11:17-18).

That happened, beginning with the decree from Cyrus. But as we read further, we realize that this prophecy is talking about more than just a return from exile. God said He will "give them one heart, and I will put a new spirit within them, and take the stony heart out of their flesh, and give them a heart of flesh, that they may walk in My statutes and keep My judgments and do them; and they shall be My people, and I will be their God" (verses 19-20). That didn't happen during the first return. That kind of commitment will not come until later.

I've always talked about near and far fulfillments, and I believe those classifications work when we're looking at the future through the prophet's eyes. But today we live in a unique time of history when more and more prophetic predictions are being realized. So I want to introduce the classifications *then*, *now*, and *soon to come*. For most prophecies about Israel there was the near fulfillment that took place back *then*. Many of them, especially the ones we are looking at in Ezekiel 36–37, also have a current "our generation" fulfillment—a *now*. But there are still more that clearly remain in the future.

For those future events, my optimism has me rejecting the indistinct "not yet," which could mean anything from one year to 1,000 years. As I take note of geopolitical shifts and the alliances being formed, and as I see Israel back in the land, thriving, and approaching a time of unprecedented peace, I feel safe in upgrading the status of Ezekiel's "not yet" prophecies to *soon to come*.

These next two chapters of Ezekiel are wonderful to read, and they include prophecies from all three categories. For many years, they were interpretive stumbling blocks, particularly to those who saw no possibility of a reconstituted Israeli nation. But for those of us in this post-1948 generation, Ezekiel 36–37 are celebrations of a God who has fulfilled His promises, is fulfilling His promises, and very soon will fulfill the rest.

Prophecies Fulfilled in Our Generation

Fulfilled Prophecy #1–Prepare the Land for Israel's Return

Most people are unaware that the great American author Mark Twain started out as a travel writer. In fact, if he were around today, he'd probably be a well-known blogger circuiting the world, making videos for his massive number of followers on YouTube, Instagram, and TikTok. Nearly a decade before he began to release classic works of fiction about Tom Sawyer and Huckleberry Finn, 32-year-old Twain took a grand adventure through Western Europe, the Baltics, Palestine, and Egypt. Two years later, in 1869, he released a book entitled *The Innocents Abroad, or The New Pilgrim's Progress*. This travel journal followed that great expedition with all the witty, descriptive, and snarky details one would expect from his brilliant pen. It's a fascinating window into the international scene of the latter nineteenth century.

As Twain passed through the Holy Land in 1867, he was wholly unimpressed with what he saw. Actually, he seemed more than unimpressed; he was disappointed. The smattering of Arab inhabitants that he came across had let the place deteriorate. The roads were nearly impassable in many areas, the sites were run down, and the whole place felt desolate.

> Of all the lands there are for dismal scenery, I think Palestine must be the prince. The hills are barren, they are dull of color, they are unpicturesque in shape. The valleys are unsightly deserts fringed with a feeble vegetation that has an expression about it of being sorrowful and despondent... Every outline is harsh, every feature is distinct, there is no perspective—distance works no enchantment here. It is a hopeless, dreary, heartbroken land...Palestine sits in sackcloth and ashes.[9]

For several chapters Twain described his sojourn in the Holy Land, and rarely was his commentary favorable. At the end of the nineteenth century, the Promised Land of Israel was in absolute ruins.

"Hey, Amir, I noticed you just skipped over the fact that Mark Twain called the land Palestine! Are you trying to cover something up?" No, I am not trying to cover anything up. And, yes, I had planned on skipping it, but since you brought it up, let's go back to where the name Palestine came from. The Roman emperor Hadrian had just quelled the second-century Bar Kokhba rebellion in Israel. Sick and tired of the troublesome Jews and wanting to give the defeated enemy a final kick in the teeth, he renamed the land *Syria Palestina*, from which we get the term *Palestine*.

The name is not some ancient title based on a mythical Palestinian people who, until recently when the nasty Jews drove them out, had filled the land with their great agriculture, technology, and commerce. There was never a Palestinian nation nor a Palestinian people. It was just a designation for people living in the area, including Jews. That's right—prior to Israel becoming a state, the Jews living in the land were known as Palestinians.

That all changed in 1948 with the birth of Israel. Suddenly, Arabs from the region took on the identity of Palestinian as a distinct people group. Never before had this term been a specific ethnic identifier.

So feel free to remove your keffiyehs, set down your placards, and send out a group text calling off the march. From the river to the sea, Palestinians aren't reality.

The Promised Land was in ruins as the nineteenth century turned into the twentieth, but God had promised a coming restoration. Through Ezekiel, He said, "You, O mountains of Israel, you shall shoot forth your branches and yield your fruit to My people Israel, for they are about to come. For indeed I am for you, and I will turn to you, and you shall be tilled and sown" (Ezekiel 36:8-9). This isn't the first time we've heard this promise. As recently as two chapters ago, Ezekiel wrote, "I will make them and the places all around My hill a blessing; and I will cause showers to come down in their season; there shall be showers of blessing. Then the trees of the field shall yield their fruit, and the earth shall yield her increase" (34:26-27).

This was the land that God had chosen for His people, and He had blessed it. That blessing is evident today. When you drive through the Galilee or down the Jordan Valley, you will see nut farms and fruit orchards galore, many producing more than one crop annually. The Jezreel, where I live, is Israel's breadbasket. Fertile fields as far as the eye can see. Every morning as I'm pouring my espresso, I look out my kitchen window and am confronted face to face with answered Bible prophecy. Ezekiel's words revealed in my own backyard!

God promised to prepare the land for the return of His people. And once that preparation began, His sheep began scampering for their home pasture.

Fulfilled Prophecy #2—Gather Israel from the Nations

The scattered people of Israel will be scattered no more. The Great Shepherd promised His flock in Ezekiel 34 that He would search for them. He said that when He found them, "[He] will bring them out from the peoples and gather them from the countries, and will bring them to their own land; [He] will feed them on the mountains of Israel, in the valleys and in all the inhabited places of the country" (verse 13).

The Jews had been scattered for 2,000 years. They were in Poland, Russia, Tunisia, France, America, Ethiopia—almost every nation you could think of had at least a few Jewish communities of one size or another. Other than the ostracization many experienced from their home countries, these people had nothing that tied them together. They had no language to unite them, their native tongue being mostly lost over the centuries. The only things that connected them were a shared history from millennia ago and long-running religious traditions.

But then suddenly, many Jews around the world began to feel a stirring in their hearts. A longing blossomed to return to the land given to their people so long ago. Sure, there had been Jews throughout the years who had trickled back to the land a few at a time. But nothing like this had happened before. Suddenly, thousands, then tens of thousands, of people poured back into their ancestral homeland. Whose hand was it that was stirring these hearts? We know the answer. "For I will take you from among the nations, gather you out of all countries, and bring you into your own land" (36:24).

A truth that I have been trying to communicate to people as I teach around the world is that Jewish people in exile are not in their natural habitat. Israel is the place God intended for them to live. Think of Nehemiah in his role as cupbearer in the royal court. Talk about a cushy job, other than the remote possibility that you might suffer a horrible death after ingesting poison intended for the king. But Nehemiah wasn't satisfied within the opulence of the palace. He had a longing to emigrate to the broken-down remains of his people's capital city, Jerusalem.

Whenever the children of Israel are ready to experience God's blessing, He draws them back to the land. That happened after the exile. It's happening again today. Statehood in 1948 changed everything. That year brought the resurrection of the Old Testament nation in which Israel once again had its own leaders and government. We are ready to receive all our people. That's why it hurts me inside to see Jews around the world representing other countries, fighting for other countries, having a life in other countries.

The great American statesman Henry Kissinger was discussing with Prime Minister Golda Meir the return of the Jews to Israel. Kissinger said to the PM, "I consider myself an American first, a secretary of state second, and a Jew third." Meir replied, "In Israel, we read from right to left."

Every year, more children of Israel are realizing that Meir was right. The numbers of those making *aliyah*, or migrating to Israel, is in the tens of thousands per annum. With each person who returns home, we are given one more example of God keeping His promises given not only through Ezekiel, but other prophets too. In Jeremiah, God said, "I will bring them back into their land which I gave to their fathers" (16:15). Through Amos, God promised:

> I will bring back the captives of My people Israel; they shall build the waste cities and inhabit them; they shall plant vineyards and drink wine from them; they shall also make gardens and eat fruit from them. I will plant them in their land, and no longer shall they be pulled up from the land I have given them (Amos 9:14-15).

This commitment was partially fulfilled after the exile. But never completely, because the people were once again pulled from the land. You and I are in the generation of this promise's realization. Finally, the people of Israel are back in the land of Israel, and there is no chance of us leaving. Even when we are facing the greatest of odds, as we'll see in chapters 38–39 of Ezekiel's book, God will be there to protect Israel and preserve the nation until the Messiah returns to rule from His throne in Jerusalem.

To emphasize His point, the Lord took Ezekiel to a valley. At some time, there had been a great battle there, and the bones of the dead were strewn across the ground. The sun and the birds had done their job removing the flesh and the gore by the time Ezekiel arrived. But it still would have been a sorrowful place. So many lives lost.

"Can these bones live?" asked the Lord (Ezekiel 37:3).

Wisely, Ezekiel passed the question back. "Lord God, You know."

Quite possibly, the prophet expected that God was going to tell him about the battle or maybe give him a new word using this killing field as a visual. Instead, the Lord treated Ezekiel to an unexpected and astounding illustration.

> Again He said to me, "Prophesy to these bones, and say to them, 'O dry bones, hear the word of the Lord! Thus says the Lord God to these bones: "Surely I will cause breath to enter into you, and you shall live. I will put sinews on you and bring flesh upon you, cover you with skin and put breath in you; and you shall live. Then you shall know that I am the Lord"'" (verses 4-6).

Ezekiel obeyed, and I don't think that any CGI animator could replicate what the prophet saw next, nor could the best audio mixer reproduce what he heard. The Lord began reuniting bone to bone, connecting them with ligaments and tendons and muscles. Organs regenerated, blood filled the veins, and a covering of flesh spread over each figure to keep everything inside. Finally, voilà, there it was! A valley filled with dead bodies! Cool trick, God, but...

> Also He said to me, "Prophesy to the breath, prophesy, son of man, and say to the breath, 'Thus says the Lord God: "Come from the four winds, O breath, and breathe on these slain, that they may live"'" (verse 9).

Again, Ezekiel obeyed. Breath filled their lungs. Hearts started beating. Blood began flowing. Brains switched back on. Eyes opened and the army stood to their feet. Stop reading and picture this scene. Incredible!

Then God told Ezekiel what all this meant:

> Son of man, these bones are the whole house of Israel. They indeed say, "Our bones are dry, our hope is lost, and we ourselves are cut off!" Therefore prophesy and say to them, "Thus says the Lord God: 'Behold, O My people, I will open your graves and cause you to come up from your graves, and bring you into the land of Israel. Then you shall know that I am the Lord, when I have opened your graves, O My people, and brought you up from your graves. I will put My Spirit in you, and you shall live, and I will place you in your own land. Then you shall know that I, the Lord, have spoken it and performed it,' says the Lord" (verses 11-14).

The people were not wrong. The once-mighty Israel was as dead as that slaughtered army. No home. No language. Nothing to unify them. But it is often when we are at our most hopeless that God shows His power. "I will open your graves…I will put My Spirit in you…I will place you in your own land." What did those bones do to regain their life? Nothing. What could God do? Everything! God put them together and reanimated them. It was His will, His decision, and His power. The people of Israel were simply the blessed, passive recipients of God's grace given to a nation that had proven over and over that it couldn't be trusted with nice things.

Not only does that resonate with me as a Jew, but as a follower of Yeshua. This death-to-life scenario is exactly what happens to every believer. Paul wrote, "God, who is rich in mercy, because of His great love with which He loved us, even when we were dead in trespasses, made us alive together with Christ (by grace you have been saved)" (Ephesians 2:4-5). Because of our sins, our spiritual bones were bleaching out in the field. But then God came along and said, "I will give you life. I will put My Spirit in you. I will bring you into My family." Praise the Lord! He has made the dead alive!

Fulfilled Prophecy #3—Rebirth of a Nation

In 1941, at the behest of Adolf Hitler, Reichsmarschall Hermann Göring sent a communication to Reinhard Heydrich asking for "an overall plan showing the preliminary organizational, substantive, and financial measures for the execution of the intended final solution of the Jewish question."[10] Second in the Schutzstaffel (SS) only to Reichsführer-SS Heinrich Himmler, Heydrich had the necessary levels of cunning and evil to carry out his task.

Plans were made and timelines created. They were submitted to and approved by Hitler, then disseminated by Heydrich to Nazi leaders at various levels of government at the 1942 Wannsee Conference. The intention was to deport 11 million Jews east from Central Europe to concentration camps. Once there, some would be executed immediately, while others would be put to forced labor so extreme that it would ensure their deaths. The plan was implemented and thousands, then millions, of Jews were slaughtered.[11]

My grandfather and grandmother on my mother's side somehow survived the Auschwitz death camp. But the experience never left them. They both lost so much family and so many friends. How can a people survive such a genocide? So many children of Israel could no longer conceive of a God who would allow such a thing to happen. But God was there. He had not turned His back on His people. As much as it grieved Him to see what was happening to His chosen ones, He had to keep His hands off because He was working a much bigger plan. We saw that plan when God said through Ezekiel,

"Behold, O My people, I will open your graves and cause you to come up from your graves, and bring you into the land of Israel. Then you shall know that I am the Lord, when I have opened your graves, O My people, and brought you up from your graves" (verses 12-13).

It took the guilt caused by the mass burial sites of so many victims to move the international community to finally vote to accept an Israeli state. This never would have happened otherwise. No people group in the world is as hated as we Jews are. It necessitated something so extraordinary, so heinous, to gather that much international support. Think about it: After the October 7, 2023, attacks, how long did it take for the world community to stop their crocodile tears over the slaughter and come after us with their marches and their resolutions and their violence? If we had lost "only" a few hundred thousand innocent lives to the Central European meat grinder, who knows whether there would be an Israel today?

Even with the millions killed during the Holocaust, only a short time passed before the United Nations turned around and began condemning Israel. And they're still doing it today. In the nine-year span from 2015 to 2023, the UN voted to condemn Israel 154 times. That works out to about one-and-a-half condemnations per month. During the same time period, that august antisemitic international body voted to condemn other countries 71 times. That's total. Israel: 154; rest of the world: 71.[12] Seems like we should qualify for a punch card or some Condemnation-of-the-Month Club.

Try as they might, the United Nations can't bring Israel down because God also provided my country with the United States. The US is quick to veto UN Security Council resolutions against Israel, and to vote no against General Assembly resolutions directed at the Jewish state. I strongly believe that is why America is the number one superpower in the world today. That's no coincidence; that's God. It all goes back to the Abrahamic covenant, when God promised that He would bless those who bless Abraham's descendants and curse those who curse them. I find myself agreeing with my fictional friend, Nir Tavor,[13] who is fond of saying that coincidence is only an excuse for those not willing to step back and see the big picture.

Through Isaiah, God asked the question, "Who has ever heard of such things? Who has ever seen things like this? Can a country be born in a day or a nation be brought forth in a moment? Yet no sooner is Zion in labor than she gives birth to her children" (Isaiah 66:8 NIV). God asked a question and answered it Himself. Then 2,700 years later, He proved His answer. On May 14, 1948, the State of Israel came into existence.

Not only was Israel reborn in a single day, it was reborn as a single nation. During the period of the kings, the country was split between north and south. Even in Jesus' time, while Samaria was located in the Roman province of Judea, it was considered a separate region from Judea itself. God had plans to remedy this.

It was time for more show-and-tell for the exiles:

> As for you, son of man, take a stick for yourself and write on it: "For Judah and for the children of Israel, his companions." Then take another stick and write on it, "For Joseph, the stick of Ephraim, and for all the house of Israel, his companions." Then join them one to another for yourself into one stick, and they will become one in your hand (Ezekiel 37:16-17).

The unification of the two sticks was to serve as a visual to the people of what God was going to do for the nation of Israel.

> Surely I will take the children of Israel from among the nations, wherever they have gone, and will gather them from every side and bring them into their own land; and I will make them one nation in the land, on the mountains

of Israel; and one king shall be king over them all; they shall no longer be two nations, nor shall they ever be divided into two kingdoms again (verses 21-22).

God's covenants were with the single nation of Israel, and His plans for the future belonged to the single nation of Israel. The sinful splitting was over. When you come to Israel today, you may hear talk about northern Israel and southern Israel. But it will only be in terms of geographical regions. We are one people of one nation, drawn from around the world. Right now, if there are divides within the country, they are political and religious. As we're finding in so many nations today, the split between conservatism and the liberal left is becoming dangerously hostile. Eventually, the issues with a runaway judicial branch are going to come to a head in some ugly way. When it comes to the divide of beliefs, the majority religion is Judaism. However, we have people of all faiths living freely in Israel. But that will one day change, and for the better.

The plan of God was not just for a physical reunion, but also a spiritual unification. The path leading to that blessed time when all will kneel before the Messiah and the incredible time of peace and joy following is found in the unfulfilled prophecies that remain in these two chapters. And God will make it all happen.

It is essential to not miss the words God uses in the passage above. Three times the word "will" is connected to the Lord's first-person pronoun. He is the One bringing them back. Quite honestly, most European Jews in the early twentieth century were not excited about coming to the Promised Land. Like Jonah, they even tried running away from God's calling.

In May 1939, many European Jews saw the Nazi buzz saw coming their way. A group of them boarded the German ship *St. Louis* in Hamburg to try to flee. But rather than seeking escape to their ancestral homeland, the 937 refugees sailed for Cuba. Sort of reminds me of the Israelites fleeing to Egypt after Jerusalem's destruction. But unlike Egypt, which accepted the Jewish survivors, Cuba refused the ship. Panicked, the passengers tried the United States and Canada. Nope and nope were the replies. With no options left, the *St. Louis* steamed back to Western Europe. Of the 937 travelers, 254 were killed in the Holocaust.

Why do people seek help from sources other than God? Cuba, the United States, and Canada were no help. In fact, they made matters worse. God said, "I will gather My people and bring them to their land." He made the promise; He accomplished His plan. Anytime there is a debate about whether the Jews belong in the land, your problem is not with the people but with God Himself.

Prophecies Unfulfilled in Our Generation
Unfulfilled Prophecy #1—A Covenant of Peace

Picture in your mind a piece of paper, perfectly white except for a smattering of black dots that mar the surface. As you examine the sheet, there seems to be no pattern to the tiny circles, no rhyme nor reason to them. But as you look more closely, you discover printed next to each dot a tiny number. Scanning the digits, you finally track down the number 1. You take your pencil, place it squarely on dot 1, and look for the one marked 2. There it is, up to the right. Dragging your pencil lead along the paper, you draw a line connecting the two points. When you've found 3, you continue your line from 2 to that next point. On and on you go until you reach the final number. Pulling back, you now find that what you took for random dots were not so random after all. When connected in the right order, they create a picture.

"Uh, thanks, Amir, for taking a whole paragraph to describe a simple connect-the-dots game. May I ask why?" Yes, of course you may. I took the time because I wanted to get into your mind the process of connecting one dot to another. This is a skill that any good biblical interpreter must possess. A passage of Scripture on its own can be a powerful thing. But when it is connected to others that bolster its truth and purpose, it can become a foundational tenet upon which we can build doctrine.

The covenant of peace was first mentioned by Ezekiel back in chapter 34. As the Lord discussed His role as the new Shepherd over Israel, He said, "I will make a covenant of peace with them, and cause wild beasts to cease from the land; and they will dwell safely in the wilderness and sleep in the woods" (verse 25). The wider context speaks of a time when there is safety from both man and beast, and there is closeness between Israel and the Lord.

In our current chapters, the Lord doubled down on this promise, saying, "Moreover I will make a covenant of peace with them, and it shall be an everlasting covenant with them" (37:26). Again, a covenant of peace, and now we learn that it is an everlasting covenant. What is this promise between God and His people? Is it a fifth covenant that we haven't spoken of yet?

This is where connecting scriptural dots is a necessity. When we do so, we'll recognize that we already know all about this covenant, only under a different name. Through Jeremiah, God said, "Behold, the days are coming, says the LORD, when I will make a new covenant with the house of Israel and with the house of Judah" (Jeremiah 31:31). The covenant of peace and the new covenant are one and the same. It, too, will be realized in a time when there is peace between Israel and the Lord due to His boundless forgiveness shown in His words, "I will forgive their iniquity, and their sin I will remember no more" (verse 34). Imagine it—sin that was great enough to cause the destruction of Jerusalem and the holy temple will be forgiven and flushed from the mind of God. Again, that is the same forgiveness promised to you and me.

But this new covenant didn't begin with Jeremiah and Ezekiel. There is another dot to connect, and that one is found in Isaiah. More than 100 years before these two prophets, Isaiah wrote of a Suffering Servant by whose "stripes we are healed" (Isaiah 53:5). Immediately following that tale of sorrow, Isaiah wrote of a marvelous promise made by God to Israel—a promise that could have been spoken just as appropriately to the audiences of the later prophets.

> "For a mere moment I have forsaken you, but with great mercies I will gather you. With a little wrath I hid My face from you for a moment; but with everlasting kindness I will have mercy on you," says the LORD, your Redeemer. "For this is like the waters of Noah to Me; for as I have sworn that the waters of Noah would no longer cover the earth, so have I sworn that I would not be angry with you, nor rebuke you. For the mountains shall depart and the hills be removed, but My kindness shall not depart from you, nor shall My covenant of peace be removed," says the LORD, who has mercy on you (54:7-10).

God brought necessary discipline, but He never removed His love. The mountains may be leveled and the hills flattened, but God's covenant with Israel will remain. Which covenant? The new covenant, the covenant of peace. When you look at Israel today, it is obvious that a final peace has not yet come between God and the children of Abraham. But the era is soon approaching when all enmity between the Lord and His people will once for all time be erased.

Unfulfilled Prophecy #2–A Fourth Temple

I am so tired of hearing about the third temple! Every single day I receive questions from people asking if the third temple is being rebuilt and where it will be placed when it is, and how will the world react, and must all the Muslims be gone for the rebuilding to happen, along with so many more! Sure, these can be intriguing queries, but for believers, they are wholly irrelevant. I won't be here to see the third temple, and hopefully you won't be either. We'll be in heaven in our resurrected bodies enjoying the physical presence of God. That is a better deal by far than checking out a fancy new building built on the Temple Mount, but which is utterly devoid of the glory of the Lord.

God promised the nation of Israel a new temple. He said:

> I will establish [Israel] and multiply them, and I will set My sanctuary in their midst forevermore. My tabernacle also shall be with them; indeed I will be their God, and they shall be My people. The nations also will know that I, the Lord, sanctify Israel, when My sanctuary is in their midst forevermore (Ezekiel 37:26-28).

The temple God speaks about in Ezekiel is an everlasting divine dwelling. It is a survivor. The third temple is not. It is one that will be established once the antichrist is revealed, and it is where he will shock all the people of Israel—who had bought into his lies—by entering the structure and declaring himself to be God.

> Let no one deceive you by any means; for that Day will not come unless the falling away comes first, and the man of sin is revealed, the son of perdition, who opposes and exalts himself above all that is called God or that is worshiped, so that he sits as God in the temple of God, showing himself that he is God (2 Thessalonians 2:3-4).

The "Day" referred to is the second coming of Christ at the end of the tribulation. This defilement of the temple will take place three-and-a-half years earlier. At that time, some of the Jews will see that they've been duped and will flee into the wilderness (Revelation 12:6).

The rest will accept this new god and ultimately, will pay for it with their lives.

This defiled third temple is short-lived, though. When the "Day" does arrive for Christ's return, the desecrated structure will be destroyed by the earthquake that emanates from the feet of the Messiah touching down on the Mount of Olives (Zechariah 14:4).

When that temple, along with the mount itself, is destroyed, it will make way for the fourth temple. This massive new house of God is often referred to as Ezekiel's temple because he goes into so much detail regarding its size and appearance. Because the prophet waits until the end of his book to dig deep into this fourth temple, we'll do the same.

Unfulfilled Prophecy #3–A King and a Kingdom

Israel has no king. I know, I live here. We have a legislature known as the Knesset, or "assembly," we have an executive body headed by the prime minister, and we have a judicial branch led by the Supreme Court. While it's true that the current Israeli Supreme Court believes itself to be made up of kings and queens, it is not actually the case. They are just power-hungry leftists who like to pretend at royalty.

It's not surprising that we have no monarchs because we are not a monarchy. Israel is not a kingdom but a unitary parliamentary republic. That's certainly not as glamorous or easy to say as kingdom, but when this system is done properly it's worked pretty well for us. Still, a time is coming when the government of Israel will shift completely. Not only will we go throwback to the days of the monarchy, but we're bringing the throwback G.O.A.T. of all kings—David himself.

> David My servant shall be king over them, and they shall all have one shepherd; they shall also walk in My judgments

and observe My statutes, and do them. Then they shall dwell in the land that I have given to Jacob My servant, where your fathers dwelt; and they shall dwell there, they, their children, and their children's children, forever; and My servant David shall be their prince forever (Ezekiel 37:24-25).

"Um, Amir, there's a slight glitch in that whole plan. I don't know how to break it to you, but David's been dead for right around 3,000 years." I hear you, and I agree that normally that could be considered a deal-breaker. However, we're talking about the life-giving God. He is the One who resurrected His Son and placed Him on the throne for all eternity. Do you really think that placing a resurrected David on the throne of Jerusalem to rule through the millennium is a big deal to Him?

Remember, all of us who have received Yeshua as our Savior and Lord will also be resurrected. And, like David, we will serve our King of kings during His 1,000-year reign. The only difference between David and us is that he knows what his job is going to be. We, on the other hand, get to experience exciting anticipation as we wait to discover the perfect job the Lord has assigned to us that will match precisely whom He has created us to be. Contrary to some popular opinion, the millennium will not just be a 1,000-year-long church service, although I'm sure there will be plenty of wonderful opportunities for worship throughout. Rather, it will be a time of serving the Lord as we, in our glorified bodies, represent Him to the surviving mortal population on Earth, which will be ever-increasing in size as the years pass.

Sadly, that flesh-bound citizenry will also gradually stray from the Lord as time goes on—to the point that there will be a ready army of rebels waiting for the devil when he is released from the abyss. The ensuing conflict will be the final one on this Earth. When it is done, the devil, his minions, and all those from all time who turned their backs on the Lord will be judged and thrown into the lake of fire. Then the Lord will create a new heaven and a new earth in which we will dwell with Him forever and ever. Then they, and we, will know that He is the Lord.

CHAPTER 11

THE GREAT EZEKIEL WAR

EZEKIEL 38-39

The servant woke up early and stretched. Dawn was beginning to break and there was much to do before his master stirred. The man he served was odd and sometimes difficult. However, he was also fair and there was no questioning his character or his virtue, so that made the stranger times a little more palatable. Slipping on his sandals, the servant tied them up quickly, grabbed a water jug, and exited the small home.

As he walked, he created a checklist for the morning. Fetch the water, feed the chickens, check the growing plants in the small garden, then prepare a breakfast for his master. The city's primary well was located near the gates, but from his location, it took only a short time to reach it. One reason he liked getting up so early was that it meant there would be a short queue. Thirty minutes of extra sleep could cost him an extra 45 minutes of wait time.

Rounding a corner, he was surprised to see no one at the well. That was a first. Dothan's water resources were limited, and he couldn't ever remember seeing an empty well during daylight hours. Then a noise caused him to look up. The wall surrounding the town was lined with people. They were frantically talking back and forth and pointing outward. Dropping his jug, the servant ran toward the wall, hustled up the stairs, then looked out. Surrounding the city, as far as he could see in both directions, was a massive army. Soldiers, horses, chariots, all prepared for battle.

"Who are they?" he exclaimed, trying to make out the insignia on the flag.

"Arameans," said a tremulous voice next to him.

The servant's heart sank. Known for their brutality and mercilessness, if the Arameans made it through the gate, there would not be one Dothanite left alive by morning. And with the size of their army and the shabbiness of the wall on which he was standing, the young man knew that there was no chance of keeping them out.

He ran. Fast as he could, he had to get home, back to his master, the prophet. Elisha was washing his face with yesterday's water when the servant burst in. Grabbing the prophet's hand, the young man tugged. "Hurry, you've got to see this! We're under attack!"

Shaking free of his servant's grip, the old prophet replied, "Attack, you say? Interesting."

After easing himself back down on his bed, he pulled his sandals closer and began the process of wrapping them onto his feet. The young man's respiratory rate increased as he shifted from one foot to the other. Elisha stood, tied his belt around his waist, then nodded toward his cloak. The servant let out an exasperated sigh before lifting it off a hook and settling it over the prophet's shoulders.

As they exited the house, it was obvious that word had spread through the town. Everyone was in a rush, screaming and running here and there. But not the old prophet. He shuffled along, stopping once to examine some apples an early riser had set up on a stand then apparently abandoned in panic. After what seemed like forever, the duo reached the top of the wall.

Pointing to the army that had begun marching toward the city, the servant cried, "Alas, my master! What shall we do?" (2 Kings 6:15). But rather than seeing terror or resignation, the servant saw peace in the prophet's eyes.

Shaking his head, the old man sighed, then replied, "Do not fear, for those who are with us are more than those who are with them" (verse 16).

The servant was confused. All he saw around him was a bunch of ragtag townspeople and a small contingent of timeworn soldiers. Then he heard the prophet praying, asking that the Lord would reveal what was really surrounding them. "Then the Lord opened the eyes of the young man, and he saw. And behold, the mountain was full of horses and chariots of fire all around Elisha" (verse 17). After some temporary blindness for the Arameans and a long walk, the enemy army was securely surrounded by their Israelite counterparts in Samaria.

As we begin these chapters on what's known by many as the Ezekiel War, we've got to remember that this realm that we live in is not all there is. It may look like Israel is just a tiny speck on our spinning globe, but that little speck is God's chosen speck. And while the combined armies of many enemy nations seem to produce impossible odds against the survival of the small nation, Israel has got a secret. The all-powerful Creator God of the universe is fighting on their side. With a friend like that, you don't need to worry about your enemy.

I know that many readers of this book have been anticipating this next event. I don't blame you; I have too. In this chapter, we're going to break down the coming Ezekiel War, looking at its timing, its players, the attack, the divine defense, and the aftermath. When this chapter comes to a close, we'll see that God's purpose in carrying out the events will be wholly accomplished. "Thus I will magnify Myself and sanctify Myself, and I will be known in the eyes of many nations. Then they shall know that I am the Lord" (Ezekiel 38:23).

The Timing—Before or After the Rapture

The number one question that I receive related to the coming Ezekiel War is whether it will take place before the rapture or after. As much as I would like to give you a definitive answer, I simply can't because there is no definitive answer given in Scripture. However, I do have a pretty good idea based on logic and reasoning.

Given the geopolitical alliances of today's world, it would be very difficult to picture anything but a post-rapture Ezekiel War. There is one primary reason for this: the United States. The commitment that Washington has made to Jerusalem makes it inconceivable that any alliance, no matter how great, would come against Israel. Economically, it would be a disaster because of the inevitable trade sanctions. These would be imposed not only by the US, but also by many other NATO countries that America would draw into its alliance. It is also conceivable, even probable, that an attack on Israel would lead to a military response that could very well turn nuclear. That is something no one wants except for some of the crazy radicals in Iran's Islamist regime.

For the Ezekiel War to take place, the US must first be neutralized. That could be achieved through some overwhelming attack by terrorists or by a foreign regime like China. However, the risks against an attacking nation are incredibly high. If the plans were found out or if the devastation was not thorough enough, the cost in retribution would be exorbitant.

A second way that the power of the US can be neutered is to just let the nation gradually deteriorate. Prior to the 2024 presidential election, America's self-deletion from relevance was moving at a rapid pace. But suddenly, the emergency brake was pulled, the car spun a 180, and a heavy dose of common sense and strength was infused back into American leadership and culture. The question is whether this will last. Will this lead to a two-year change, a four-year change, or a more long-lasting revitalization of traditional values? If this renewal of sanity turns out to simply be a blip in the downward slide of America, then it won't be too long before Israel will be on its own.

The third, and what I believe to be the most likely, possibility for causing the US to fall off its number one seat on the world stage is for the rapture to occur. There is no other nation on Earth that will experience the same level of internal wreckage due to the astonishing number of people who will disappear in a single moment. A quick search on the internet will provide you with a widespread range of percentages relating to the number of evangelical Christians in America. By "evangelical," I'm talking about the true born-again, Spirit-filled believers in Jesus Christ who will take flight in the rapture. Optimistic polls say as many as 30 to 35 percent, which seems very high to me. On the more pessimistic side, there are those who say less than 10 percent.

Just for the sake of argument, let's go with an especially low number of one in twenty Americans being truly saved. With a population of just under 350 million,[14] that would mean that 17.5 million believers would suddenly vanish from the populace. The US would absolutely shut down. Think of what happened when COVID hit, and, by the loosest definitions, 1.2 million died over a four-year-period.[15] Businesses, food supply, entertainment, and everything else you can think of came to a screeching halt. Well, all except for government, which went into hyperdrive.

If instead of less than half a percent dying over four years you have 5 percent or more gone instantaneously, the US will immediately fall from its position as a world player, at least for a time. There will be way too much for the nation to do to try to get its legs back under itself. That will open the door for other nations to carry out the secret plans they've had neatly stored away in a file cabinet marked "For When the United States Collapses." China will immediately take over Taiwan, then sweep through the Eastern Pacific.

The Philippines, Japan, Indonesia, and possibly even Australia will all come under Beijing's sway.

While that's going on, Russia will make a pact with China, essentially saying, "You do your thing over there and we'll do ours over here." Then they'll gather the allies they already have today—Turkey, Iran, and a few others—and will put into action a plan for Israel they've had waiting for such a time as this.

The Timing—Confusion with Revelation 20

A second question I also receive has to do with conflating the Ezekiel War with the great final battle of Revelation 20. It's an understandable mistake given the name of the primary antagonist.

> Now the word of the LORD came to me, saying, "Son of man, set your face against Gog, of the land of Magog, the prince of Rosh, Meshech, and Tubal, and prophesy against him, and say, 'Thus says the Lord GOD: "Behold, I am against you, O Gog, the prince of Rosh, Meshech, and Tubal"'" (Ezekiel 38:1-3).

The prophecy was addressed to Gog of the land of Magog. But that isn't the only time we hear of this Gog. At the end of the millennium, Satan will be released from the abyss and he "will go out to deceive the nations which are in the four corners of the earth, Gog and Magog, to gather them together to battle, whose number is as the sand of the sea" (Revelation 20:8). If Gog of Magog appears to be defeated before the tribulation according to Ezekiel 38, then why are we seeing him 1,007 years later, give or take a few years? Is it possible that the Ezekiel War could really be referring to that final battle before the end of the world?

No, it's not. First, the battle in Ezekiel comes primarily from the north and involves only a few nations (Ezekiel 38:6, 15; 39:2). The battle in Revelation 20:7-9 will draw in all nations coming from all directions. Second, while Satan is undoubtedly involved behind the scenes in the Ezekiel War, Revelation 20:8 places him out front leading the charge. Third, Ezekiel said that after his namesake war,

> It will come to pass in that day that I will give Gog a burial place there in Israel, the valley of those who pass by east of the sea; and it will obstruct travelers, because there they will bury Gog and all his multitude. Therefore they will call it the Valley of Hamon Gog. For seven months the house of Israel will be burying them, in order to cleanse the land (39:11-12).

This makes sense if the land is to be purified for further use. But immediately following the Revelation 20 war is the Great White Throne judgment, which is then succeeded by the creation of a new heavens and a new earth. Cleaning up, then, would be akin to straightening the deck chairs on the Titanic.

Scripturally, it's clear that Ezekiel 38–39 and Revelation 20 are talking about two different events. So why the similar names? In Revelation 20, rather than Gog being the name of a specific person, it refers to a spirit and attitude of rebellion against God. That's not to say that "Gog, the prince of Rosh, Meshech, and Tubal" could not also be a person who represents that rebellious spirit. However, I doubt that you'll find that three-letter name on his driver's license.

The forces coming out of the far north in Ezekiel 38 are rising up to destroy the children of Israel, God's people. In Revelation 20, Satan is making a last futile effort to take down God Himself. In both cases, there is rebellion against God. And in both cases, Gog is defeated.

Who's Who–the Bad Guys

A coalition of enemies is journeying down toward Israel. Some are easy to identify, but others take a little more work to figure out.

To get an idea of who we're talking about, we need to go all the way back to the flood. When God washed the world clean, he saved Noah and his family, which included one wife, three daughters-in-law, and three sons, Shem, Ham, and Japheth. Noah and his sons were given the mandate, "Be fruitful and multiply, and fill the earth" (Genesis 9:1). Unfortunately, they liked it where they were. Lush greenery, strong tower-building soil. So the Lord mixed up their language and the people scattered. The descendants of Shem went south to Arabia and Asia. The children of Ham also went south, but they kept going all the way to Africa. Japheth, though, went north and west. When we look at the names of his sons and grandsons, we'll see a few that fit into our story now.

> The sons of Japheth were Gomer, Magog, Madai, Javan, Tubal, Meshech, and Tiras. The sons of Gomer were Ashkenaz, Riphath, and Togarmah (10:2-3).

We already met Gog of Magog, the prince of Rosh, Meshech, and Tubal above. This leader will travel down to invade the nation of Israel, and he'll be bringing friends.

> I will turn you around, put hooks into your jaws, and lead you out, with all your army, horses, and horsemen, all splendidly clothed, a great company with bucklers and shields, all of them handling swords. Persia, Ethiopia, and Libya are with them, all of them with shield and helmet; Gomer and all its troops; the house of Togarmah from the far north and all its troops—many people are with you (Ezekiel 38:4-6).

On first glance, it seems quite easy to determine the location of Magog. Rosh sounds a lot like Russia. A case could be made for

Meshech being Moscow. And as for Tubal, could it maybe be Tobolsk, that smallish city located way east above Kazakhstan? Maybe, but maybe not. I'm not denying that Gog refers to a Russian leader. I'd just like stronger evidence.

In Ezekiel 39, when God told Gog once again that He was going to lead the prince down to Israel, He added one more detail. "Behold, I am against you, O Gog, the prince of Rosh, Meshech, and Tubal; and I will turn you around and lead you on, bringing you up from the far north, and bring you against the mountains of Israel" (verses 1-2). Where is Gog being led from? The far north. What country is to the far north of Israel? Russia. So geographically, this makes sense.

One more source lends credence to this Gog and Magog connection to Russia. Josephus, the first-century Jewish historian, equated these two entities with the Scythians who lived north of the Caspian Sea. These warlike people caused so much trouble from the eighth through the third centuries BC that Alexander the Great supposedly built a wall to keep them from invading into his territory. The name of this great barrier? The wall of Magog.

"Um, Amir, did I just see a 'supposedly' in that last piece of evidence?" Alas, you did. The reason is because the historical confirmation of the wall is not at the level that I would call a sure thing. Also, Josephus, while a great source for the feel of a historical time period, is not always 100 percent accurate on the details. That is why I relegate this to the "lends credence" category, instead of the "is evidence" list.

Dr. John F. Walvoord, former president and chancellor of Dallas Theological Seminary, sums up the argument for a Russian Magog:

> The only nation that the description "far north" would fit would be Russia, which, of course, is to the north of Israel, with Moscow being directly north of Jerusalem. Though some attempt to question the identification, because Russia extends more than six thousand miles east and west, any

reference to a nation to the far north of Israel would have to be Russia because of the geographic facts involved.[16]

From what we know of Russia—its military strength, its expansionist ideologies, and its overwhelming desire for energy—it is the perfect fit for Magog, where are located Rosh, Meshech, and Tubal.

Then there is the rest of the alliance. Persia is Iran. Ethiopia is a translation of the Hebrew word *Cush* and is centered on Sudan. *Put* is the next country, which the NKJV accurately translates as Libya. Gomer and the house of Togarmah, or Beth-Togarmah, are both part of Turkey. It's true that Togarmah is also referred to as "the far north." But Turkey is just a Baltic Sea or a small country of Georgia away from Russia, depending on where you're looking. All of it is far north of Israel.

What we gather from the Lord's words is that an axis of evil made up from countries to the north, east, and west of Israel will form with the intent of destroying the Jewish nation. It's interesting to note that for the first time in Israel's history, it will only be second-tier countries that will attack. No nations along Israel's borders will be part of this attempted invasion. Lebanon, Syria, and possibly Jordan will possess the land that the attack will come from. However, the nations themselves will not be participants.

The question remains why these powers, particularly the three main players, would be so intent on invading and destroying Israel. The answer is not complicated, especially if you understand who these nations are. For Russia, their purpose is power, and that is in two senses. First, they are an energy economy. Israel is cutting in on their revenues with massive natural gas fields located just off the Mediterranean coast. Russia covets the fields and needs to reclaim their former customers that Israel is now supplying. Second, the Soviet Union used to be on par with America in strength and begrudged respect. That is no longer true, especially with the current status of the war with Ukraine. That may change by the time this book is published, but right now, both sides are taking heavy losses, and both are looking for a dignified way out. If Russia becomes the major player in the Middle East by leading this take-down of Israel, it can resume its place as one of world's superpowers.

For Iran, the purpose is revenge. The Islamist regime in Tehran has experienced one humiliation after another from Israel. From bombings to targeted killings to having their nuclear secrets stolen to having their nuclear facilities sabotaged, it is always the ayatollahs with egg on their face. They're done with all this, and they want payback in the worst way. I'm fully expecting that by the time this book is published, Iran's nuclear program will have been dealt with one way or another.

Turkey has been considered the sick man of Europe for decades. The Ottoman Empire is no more, and Turkey is a shell of what it once was. The purpose for Turkey's participation in this military endeavor is respect. They don't want to be snickered at anymore when their backs are turned. As one of the leads in taking down Israel, they will attempt to garner the prestige they once enjoyed, particularly within the Muslim world. A successful attack also won't be bad for Turkey's financial bottom line, which is essentially trashed right now.

Who's Who—the Onlookers

An unexpected development has taken place in the last decade. Isolated Israel has made friends with some of its neighbors. Thanks to the efforts behind the United States's Abraham Accords, walls began to break down between the Jewish state and some nearby moderate Muslim countries. Morocco, Bahrain, and the United Arab Emirates have all forged reasonable relations with Israel. Saudi Arabia is walking the fine line of furled brows in front with an arm of semi-friendship hidden around the waist in back. This forging of camaraderie is a necessary step for the Ezekiel War to take place, because when the invasion comes, moderate Sunni Muslims are going to be asking the Axis of Evil, "What in the world are you guys doing?"

> Sheba, Dedan, the merchants of Tarshish, and all their young lions will say to you, "Have you come to take plunder? Have you gathered your army to take booty, to carry away silver and gold, to take away livestock and goods, to take great plunder?" (38:13-14).

This will be a first. One Muslim nation asking another Muslim nation, "Why are you messing with Israel?"

Sadly, their criticism won't go beyond words. Most people have their work friends and their friend friends. Their work friends are the ones they'll joke with around the water cooler and team up with for a job. But if you're having a special-occasion party at your house, they aren't the ones who will be getting an invitation. Those are reserved for your friend friends, the ones you really like and who you spend time with because you want to, not because you both happened to have been hired by the same HR department. Israel is making friends, but they're work friends. Chances are they won't be invited over to any Saudi's *Eid al-Fitr* party anytime soon. The verbal admonishments against the Axis may be harsh, but verbal they will remain.

There are still the merchants of Tarshish and all their young lions to identify. The merchants most likely belong to Europe. When the Ezekiel War approaches, they'll yell and stomp their feet, but the Russian coalition knows their Western neighbors' United Nations voting records. They'll recognize that they have nothing to worry about from the Europeans as far as Israel is concerned. A good case can be made for Europe's young lions being the United States. Born out of Europe, there is certainly a familial relationship. Unfortunately for Israel, as we saw earlier, the US will be too busy trying to keep its head above water to lend a helping hand.

The Attack

The world will be in upheaval. Millions of people will have just disappeared, the number one superpower will be reeling from a near-knockout blow, many other countries will have lost citizens to one extent or another to the great vanishing, and people will wonder whether they've been visited by aliens or if some wild new pandemic is stealing others away. In other words, civilization will be going crazy. *What an opportune time*, the Russian president will think, *to launch an invasion*.

His executive secretary will set up a conference call with the Supreme Leader of Iran, the president of Turkey, and the leaders of Sudan and Libya. The Russian president will tell them:

> I will go up against a land of unwalled villages; I will go to a peaceful people, who dwell safely, all of them dwelling without walls, and having neither bars nor gates—to take plunder and to take booty, to stretch out [my] hand against the waste places that are again inhabited, and against a people gathered from the nations, who have acquired livestock and goods, who dwell in the midst of the land (38:11-12).

Then he'll add, "Wanna come along?"

Before you know it, there is a massive army pushing down through Syria and Lebanon toward Israel's northern border. Meanwhile, the combined air forces of the nations are landing at Syrian and Lebanese military bases and their navies are flooding the Mediterranean off Israel's coast. This coming war is not going to be settled with an air offensive or a nuclear strike. This is a ground invasion designed to make October 7 pale in comparison.

There will be nothing subtle about the buildup to war. "Then you will come from your place out of the far north, you and many peoples with you, all of them riding on horses, a great company and a mighty army. You will come up against My people Israel like a cloud, to cover the land" (verses 15-16). Israel will be helpless. Their only option would be to go nuclear, but with the buildup right on their borders, doing so would be incredibly dangerous to their own people and land. Besides, with the proximity of the massive nuclear arsenal of Russia, the small nation of Israel would cease to exist in a matter of minutes. All that's left to the Israelis will be to shake in their boots as they await the attack.

Or could there be more? If there is one thing that the Jewish people know through and through, it is the Tanakh, aka the Old Testament. I'm not saying that all Israelis know it, but enough do to ensure that a connection will be made with the Ezekiel War. The acceptance of this event as a fulfillment of prophecy may start small at first, but as the odds against Israel grow worse and worse, the number of prayers for God's intervention will grow greater and greater.

Soon, it will become evident to all, both inside Israel and to those watching from the outside—Sheba, Dedan, and the rest of the world—that only a miracle from God can save Israel. God prophesied to Gog, "You will come up against My people Israel like a cloud, to cover the land. It will be in the latter days that I will bring you against My land, so that the nations may know Me, when I am hallowed in you, O Gog, before their eyes" (verse 16). In other words, "When the world sees Me crush you, then they will know that I am the Lord."

The Defense

The battle lines are drawn. Any countermeasures Israel tried will have had no effect. Zero hour has come. Engines roar to life. Tanks, military transports, jet fighters, UAVs, bombers, all ready to go. In the Mediterranean, a final check is given to the missile systems of each warship, and the fighters and attack helicopters scream awake. The signal is given, and the seemingly unstoppable army will rumble across the border, unaware that it is about to barrel head-on into an immovable force.

At first, all will seem to be going just as planned as the combined armies drive through and level abandoned town after abandoned town in northern Israel. Once Gog's confidence is at its highest, God will step into the picture.

> "It will come to pass at the same time, when Gog comes against the land of Israel," says the Lord GOD, "that My fury will show in My face. For in My jealousy and in the fire of My wrath I have spoken: 'Surely in that day there shall be a great earthquake in the land of Israel, so that the fish of the sea, the birds of the heavens, the beasts of the field, all creeping things that creep on the earth, and all men who are on the face of the earth shall shake at My presence. The mountains shall be thrown down, the steep places shall fall, and every wall shall fall to the ground.' I will call for a sword against Gog throughout all My mountains," says the Lord GOD. "Every man's sword will be against his brother. And I will bring him to judgment with pestilence and bloodshed; I will rain down on him, on his troops, and on the many peoples who are with him, flooding rain, great hailstones, fire, and brimstone. Thus I will magnify Myself and sanctify Myself, and I will be known in the eyes of many nations. Then they shall know that I am the LORD" (38:18-23).

This is not an allegory. It is not a word picture. There are no uses of the words *like* or *likeness* in this narrative. You are reading exactly what will happen. An earthquake, murderous confusion with brother killing brother, deadly disease, floods, massive hail, and a return of Sodom and Gomorrah-like fire and brimstone.

Many of today's interpreters try to find modern equivalents to these methods of death. "The pestilence refers to chemical weapons. Fire and brimstone is talking about cluster bombs and other ordnance." I strongly disagree. It's true that we need to upgrade the modes of transportation. If you think describing a cherub threw Ezekiel off, try having him detail out a MiG-35. But there is no reason to "interpret up" the destruction. If it was Israel's weaponry that destroyed the Axis of Evil, then the rest of the world would say, "Those Israelis! Somehow they pulled it off again!" But fire and brimstone falling from the sky? "Then they shall know that I am the Lord!"

One last item: Notice who is not on the receiving end of this destruction? "Every man's sword will be against his brother." "I will rain down on [Gog], on his troops, and on the many peoples who are with him." Undoubtedly, the people of Israel will get plenty bounced around during the earthquake, but the only ones affected by these destroying divine weapons are Gog and his allies. That clear distinction will cement the truth in everyone's mind that it was the Lord God who brought this victory.

Aftermath in Israel

When the sulfur smoke from the brimstone clears, it's time to get out the shovels.

> It will come to pass in that day that I will give Gog a burial place there in Israel, the valley of those who pass by east of the sea; and it will obstruct travelers, because there they will bury Gog and all his multitude. Therefore they will call it the Valley of Hamon Gog. For seven months the house of Israel will be burying them, in order to cleanse the land (39:11-12).

What a job! Seven months of burying the dead. But the people of

Israel will be diligent and efficient and "will gain renown" for their efforts (verse 13).

It's not just the bodies that will need removal, it's also the weapons of war. The Lord spoke of weapons being burned for fuel, which could be an anachronism, or it could refer the weapons being melted down for fuel of some type. Possibly the steel could be used for making wind turbines or parts for solar fields. That's one of those questions we'll need to leave hanging out there, knowing that one day the meaning will be clear.

The destruction of the Axis of Evil is complete. Russia is devastated. Iran and radical Islam are devastated. Turkey is devastated. The United States remains devastated from the rapture. This will leave China as the number one superpower in the world. Imagine Europe realizing that it is just one extremely long, unmanned Russian highway away from the PRC rolling in and setting up shop in Switzerland or Austria. The only hope that the Europeans will have to stand against them is by banding together. An iron-strong bond will need to form that will unify the nations into one unit, much like the states did in America.

It will be out of that unified Europe that a man will assert himself. After so much war, he will be a man of peace. And after the attempted destruction of Israel, there is one gift that he can give to the nation that will show that he truly is the man who can bring all people together. He will negotiate a deal for the third temple to be built on the Temple Mount. The world will be amazed at his brilliance, and the Israeli people will swoon at his feet.

This gullibility of the Israelis will be because messianic aspirations will be through the roof. They will have seen the power of God protecting them in a supernatural way. This will boost their expectations of a soon-coming, post-Ezekiel War Messiah to such a level that they will be ready to lay the title on any man with two arms, two legs, and a land deed for a third temple.

Once the temple is built, Israel will want nothing more than to reup the sacrificial system so that people can once again offer sacrifices to the Lord. As the Lord put it, "So I will make My holy name known in the midst of My people Israel, and I will not let them profane My holy name anymore. Then the nations shall know that I am the Lord, the Holy One in Israel" (verse 7). But despite the promise made by God later in chapter 39, where He said, "I will not hide My face from them anymore; for I shall have poured out My Spirit on the house of Israel" (verse 29), that day is not yet. Israel may have taken a step in God's direction, but it is not directly toward Him. In that day, the people will glory over a temple, but not over the Messiah. They will rejoice over a building, but not over the One it represents.

As the next three-and-a-half years pass, the harrowing experience of the attack will begin to fade in the minds of many Israelis. I can perfectly picture this happening because I've already seen it in some of the inane compromises members of our government and our courts want to make with Hamas today. The temple sacrifices will continue, but fewer and fewer people will care. The novelty will wear off. Besides, they'll think, *There's that amazing guy who got the temple built. He's the one our eyes need to be on.*

Then, one day, that guy will step into the temple and reveal a new object of worship—a statue of himself. Two-thirds of the world's Jews will either go along with this new antichrist worship, or they just won't care. One-third, however, will realize that they've made a horrible mistake. Panicking, they will flee into the wilderness, where God will supernaturally take care of them for three-and-a-half years despite the fact that they still reject His Son.

When the full seven years of God's discipline of Israel and His judgment on the world are complete, Yeshua the Messiah will return to the Mount of Olives. All the remaining Jews from around the world will gather before Him. In that moment, they will realize not only who the Messiah is, but they will recognize God's plan. The Messiah had to come and He had to die. But then, with Him standing there before them, they will also realize that death couldn't hold Him. He rose again, then ascended into heaven, waiting for this very moment to reveal Himself to them.

A light bulb will burst to life in their brains and in their hearts. They will realize that they had been so wrong for so long. They will mourn for Him, pouring out their repentance. They will confess their sins, receive Him as their Savior and Lord, and so all Israel will be saved.

Up until the end, God will never forget His children. He will never back out on a covenant. Even when His people were at their most rebellious before the exile, He loved them and cared for them. When Gog and his armies come against the unbelieving nation of Israel, God will protect His people. When the antichrist shows his true colors and begins slaughtering the Jews, God will protect the believing and the unbelieving remnant of global Jews. And when the period of discipline is finally and completely over, He will take their hearts of stone, give them a heart of flesh, accept their confessions, forgive their sins, and bring them into His kingdom.

CHAPTER 12

THE RETURN OF THE KING

EZEKIEL 40-48

There's bad stuff. There's really bad stuff. Then, there's really, really bad stuff. One of the many qualities to love about Ezekiel is that, despite having to deal with the bad and the really bad, we get to skip most of the really, really bad.

That really, really bad is the tribulation that will come after the rise of the antichrist. We've touched on that servant of Satan and the seven years of discipline and punishment that will follow his ascension into world prominence and admiration. We've briefly discussed the terrible destruction and suffering that will be wrought upon the earth and its population through the seal, trumpet, and bowl judgments. It is all very good information for believers to understand, even though we won't be around to experience any of the terrors. We'll have been raptured prior to Daniel's prophesied "week" of wrath.

But for this study, we don't need to delve into the tribulation horrors. This is Ezekiel's book, and the prophet has seen fit to skip the years of Jacob's trouble. As soon as the war is finished, we jump right to the millennium. If you want to learn more about the tribulation, I have other books that will give you all the information you want.

Measuring the Temple (40–42)

"Ugh, Amir, is there any chance we can skip the next few chapters? It's all just Ezekiel and a guy with a stick measuring a new temple. Can't we just say that the rebuilt worship center is really big, then move on?" Trust me, I understand where you are coming from. On the surface, these next chapters look like a guaranteed snoozefest. But remember, God put them in here for a loftier reason than simply allowing us to skim through one day's Bible reading in record time. Besides, you might find yourself a lot more interested than you expect. So, drop a double caffeine capsule into your Nespresso machine and let's get down to business.

Ezekiel began the description of his vision with a partial time stamp.

> In the twenty-fifth year of our captivity, at the beginning of the year, on the tenth day of the month, in the fourteenth year after the city was captured, on the very same day the hand of the LORD was upon me; and He took me there. In the visions of God He took me into the land of Israel and set me on a very high mountain; on it toward the south was something like the structure of a city. He took me there, and behold, there was a man whose appearance was like the appearance of bronze. He had a line of flax and a measuring rod in his hand, and he stood in the gateway (Ezekiel 40:1-3).

The year was 573 BC, 14 years after Jerusalem fell. The prophet was in his forties and had been a widow for more than a decade and a half. His life in the interval is somewhat of a mystery. What was his daily routine? Was he still prophesying regularly? Had he taken up his role as a priest, or was he still a lonely hermit who occasionally stepped outside to tell people to straighten up their acts?

Whatever Ezekiel's day-to-day looked like, God chose an opportune time to interrupt it. Suddenly, he was taken up and carried to a high mountain overlooking Jerusalem. The city below him, however, was not the Jerusalem he remembered from before he was stolen away. It was also not the series of ruins he knew currently inhabited the site.

Spread out in front of Ezekiel was a beautifully rebuilt city with a huge temple complex. A throat cleared next to him, and he turned to see a bronze-looking man prepared to measure the enormous holy site. Before the man began his task, he gave Ezekiel a charge, saying, "Son of man, look with your eyes and hear with your ears, and fix your mind on everything I show you; for you were brought here so that I might show them to you. Declare to the house of Israel everything you see" (verse 4). Watch, listen, learn, pass it on. After his 20-plus years of prophesying, that was one series of tasks that he had down pat.

The measuring began:

> Now there was a wall all around the outside of the temple. In the man's hand was a measuring rod six cubits long, each being a cubit and a handbreadth; and he measured the width of the wall structure, one rod; and the height, one rod (verse 5).

Hey, I see the glaze already passing across your eyes! But don't feel bad; nobody else has any idea what a cubit is either. Even Old Testament theologians refill their coffee mugs at this point and think, *Oy, this is going to be a grind.*

Measurements in Scripture can be difficult. No one knows anymore what a hin or an ephah or a talent was. When Ezekiel talks about a six-cubit-long rod, he may be talking about something massive or something incredibly small. Only a certified master in cubitology would know!

I'm going to let you into "Amir's Little Cheatcode for Cubiting." On your phone or computer, do a search for www.biblegateway.com. Once there, on the version menu to the right, select New Living Translation (NLT). Then type in a search for Ezekiel 40. Voila! Suddenly, the math is all done for you. Now the passage reads:

> I could see a wall completely surrounding the Temple area. The man took a measuring rod that was 10½ feet long and measured the wall, and the wall was 10½ feet thick and 10½ feet high (verse 5 NLT).[17]

If you aren't a fan of biblical paraphrases, no problem! Just read from whatever version you normally use and keep the NLT open for reference. It's so much easier to picture a square courtyard with sides of 175 feet than of 100 cubits. By the way, this interpretation hack works for most other units of measurement too.

The survey began at the Eastern Gate, which was significant because that was the one used when the glory of the Lord departed the temple. It is likely the gate that Jesus entered on Palm Sunday as He rode in westward from the Mount of Olives. The Eastern Gate is also the passage that the glory of the Lord will use when He returns in Ezekiel 43.

This whole section presents a dilemma. Just how deep do we go when it comes to the measurements? My philosophy in this book, as it was in *Revealing Revelation* and *Discovering Daniel*, is to familiarize the reader with a part of the Bible that is often a black hole to the everyday Christian. Therefore, I purposely don't get too far down into the weeds. In other words, we get deep, but we don't get commentary deep. Because of that, I'm going to let Ezekiel and his companion take their measurements, and I'll offer some opportunities in this book's workbook for you to dig a little further down should you desire.

There are two reasons given to Ezekiel for taking these measurements.

Reason #1–The Shame of Israel

When this prophecy came to Ezekiel, there was no temple in Jerusalem. But there would be soon. Sadly, it would pale in comparison to the first temple's glory. When the foundations for the post-exilic temple had been laid by the returnees, all the younger folk cheered their progress. But for the older ones who had seen Solomon's structure, it was a time of mourning.

> All the people shouted with a great shout, when they praised the LORD, because the foundation of the house of the LORD was laid. But many of the priests and Levites and heads of the fathers' houses, old men who had seen the first temple, wept with a loud voice when the foundation of this temple was laid before their eyes (Ezra 3:11-12).

Once the words of Ezekiel's prophecy were heard, there would be even more shame. Not only was their second temple going to be overshadowed by the first, but it would be downright embarrassing when compared to the temple of the millennium.

> Son of man, describe the temple to the house of Israel, that they may be ashamed of their iniquities; and let them measure the pattern. And if they are ashamed of all that they have done, make known to them the design of the temple and its arrangement, its exits and its entrances, its entire design and all its ordinances, all its forms and all its laws (Ezekiel 43:10-11).

Ezekiel was to first give the people the basic outline of the temple that was to come. The result would likely be shame and regret when they compared its future grandeur to what stood in front of them. But God didn't want to leave them down in the dumps. These men were trying to get things right with God. Yes, they were paying a heavy price, and the diminutive new temple was evidence. But a time would come when a massive, majestic new temple would be built with all the beauty and intricacies involved in such a place of worship. A city that had a temple like that had to be a great city indeed. The people could be encouraged by the fact that a time was coming when Jerusalem would once again be fully rebuilt and respected amongst the nations.

Reason #2–The Holiness of God

The future temple and its grounds were laid out in such a way as to communicate the holiness of the Lord. The temple itself was extremely large—875 feet by 875 feet. Surrounding the temple grounds would be a beautifully tended open area of 87.5 feet stretching out on all sides. And there's more.

A sacred area will be created within which the temple will sit. Like a city inside a city, "this piece of land will be 8⅓ miles long and 6⅔ miles wide. The entire area will be holy" (45:1 NLT). This piece of land will also be divided in half by width.

> Within the larger sacred area, measure out a portion of land 8⅓ miles long and 3⅓ miles wide. Within it the sanctuary of the Most Holy Place will be located. This area will be holy, set aside for the priests who minister to the LORD in the sanctuary. They will use it for their homes, and my Temple will be located within it. The strip of sacred land next to it, also 8⅓ miles long and 3⅓ miles wide, will be a living area for the Levites who work

at the Temple. It will be their possession and a place for their towns (verses 3-5 NLT).

In one half of the sacred area will sit the temple surrounded by the dwellings of its priests. The other half is full of Levites, who also work at the temple, carrying out all the holy tasks that don't involve actual worship.

The word "holy" means to be "set apart." This enormous temple complex will be a visual for all that God isn't just another guy living in a single-story ranch at the end of the cul-de-sac. He is the Creator of all things, Almighty of the universe, and His house will show it. Not only will the grandeur of the building communicate His glory, but the grounds themselves will ensure that everyone around the world understands His otherness.

The Glory of the Lord Returns (43–48)

When the exiles returned to Jerusalem, they were determined to build the new temple. They laid the foundations in 538 BC, but then ran into trouble. Political pressure caused them to stop, and the temple grounds lay dormant for more than 18 years. Out of sight, out of mind. People had enough trouble just starting their lives back up.

Soon enough, though, God got tired of being ignored and sent the prophets Zechariah and Haggai to light a fire under the returnees. While Zechariah's prophecies leaned toward the fantastic and slightly bizarre, Haggai delivered his messages with typical Jewish bluntness. God gave him a message for Zerubbabel the governor and Joshua the high priest and to all the others regarding their hibernating attempt at building a new temple. "Who is left among you who saw this temple in its former glory? And how do you see it now? In comparison with it, is this not in your eyes as nothing?" (Haggai 2:3). Wow, Haggai, little harsh, don't you think? Maybe, but it was true.

God didn't just rub it in and leave them dejected. He promised that a very special future was in store for the returnees' second temple.

> Thus says the Lord of hosts: "Once more (it is a little while) I will shake heaven and earth, the sea and dry land; and I will shake all nations, and they shall come to the Desire of All Nations, and I will fill this temple with glory," says the Lord of hosts. "The silver is Mine, and the gold is Mine," says the Lord of hosts. "The glory of this latter temple shall be greater than the former," says the Lord of hosts. "And in this place I will give peace," says the Lord of hosts (verses 6-9).

Here, we come to another prophecy with a near and far fulfillment. The near fulfillment would take place more than 500 years after Haggai's pronouncement. By that time, the second temple would have received a major expansion and facelift from Herod the Great. The glory of the Lord would return and fill the temple, and that glory would outshine that which had filled the first temple.

How is that possible? The Lord Himself would physically enter this Temple 2.0 and would teach and touch and show love to all who would turn their eyes to Him. He would even continue His heartbroken and long-suffering love toward those who turned their backs on Him and eventually nailed Him to a cross. Jesus walked the stones of the second temple, and thus made its glory even greater than that of the former.

But that wasn't the end. As amazing as that fulfillment was, one even greater was coming. As Ezekiel watched his vision play out, he once again saw the glory of the Lord coming back the way it had departed. From the east it approached, "and the earth shone with His glory" (Ezekiel 43:2). On its arrival, the Spirit carried the prophet into the temple, and he watched as the glory of the Lord once again filled the temple. Then God spoke to Ezekiel:

> Son of man, this is the place of My throne and the place of the soles of My feet, where I will dwell in the midst of the children of Israel forever. No more shall the house of Israel defile My holy name, they nor their kings, by their harlotry or with the carcasses of their kings on their high places. When they set their threshold by My threshold, and their doorpost by My doorpost, with a wall between them and Me, they defiled My holy name by the abominations which they committed; therefore I have consumed them in My anger. Now let them put their harlotry and the carcasses of their kings far away from Me, and I will dwell in their midst forever (verses 7-9).

Some will debate whether this is referring to the first, second, third, or fourth temple. The word "forever" answers the question. Twice in this passage the Lord uses that time reference to indicate that He will never leave His people again. There will be no more "glory leaving the temple." Earlier in Ezekiel, we watched as the cloud rose and departed through the Eastern Gate. In the second temple, the glory came for a brief time in the person of Jesus Christ, but then left once again. The glory was nowhere near the third temple during the tribulation. That temple will be a deception used by the antichrist to gain power and accolades. This leaves us with the fourth temple—the millennial temple. For the rest of the time that this world exists, God's glory will always remain in this final temple.

It's true that a moment will come when this heaven and earth will end, only to be remade anew. In that new creation, there will be no need for a temple. John the Revelator gave the explanation for its absence, saying that "the Lord God Almighty and the Lamb are its temple" (Revelation 21:22). Why do you need a building to represent the presence of the Godhead when the Father and the Son will be there with you?

There is so much more to these last few chapters. We could easily get caught up in the details and emerge some hundred pages later. So I am going to pull back on our zoom just a bit and wrap up our book with four final issues.

Final Issue #1—What's with the Sacrificial System?

The concern begins following the return of the glory of the Lord. God proclaims a process of sacrifices, including sin offerings for the priests and purification and dedication offerings for the altar. "'Seven days they shall make atonement for the altar and purify it, and so consecrate it. When these days are over it shall be, on the eighth day and thereafter, that the priests shall offer your burnt offerings and your peace offerings on the altar; and I will accept you,' says the Lord GOD" (Ezekiel 43:26-27).

I know exactly what you're thinking, so I'll say it for you. "Um, Amir, if Jesus died once for all sins for all time, why is God receiving sin offerings in the millennium?" Great question, if I do say so myself. This conundrum has had theologians doing somersaults and standing on their heads for centuries. It also has amillennialists pointing their fingers, saying, "See! This can't refer to a real thousand-year period. Otherwise, you're saying that Israel is restoring the Mosaic system of sacrifice, which would be blasphemous!" My response to them is, "Relax. I understand your concern. Now, let's have a cup of tea and look at why this actually makes a lot of sense."

First, we need to remember that Israel and the church are not the same. I know that some replacement theology people are reeling at that statement, but it's true. I don't have time to get into it here, but you can check out my books *The Israel Decree* and *Israel and the Church* for detailed explanations as to why that is a biblically accurate statement.

Despite Israel and the church being two separate entities, there are some who believe that at the second coming, when Paul said that "all

Israel will be saved" (Romans 11:26), Israel will then become part of the church. After all, isn't the true church synonymous with being a Christian? You receive Jesus, you are given eternal life, and within five to seven business days, you receive a membership card for entrance into your local denomination.

However, that timing doesn't work out. At the rapture, the church age ends. The Holy Spirit is removed as the Restrainer, and His responsibility of indwelling every believer comes to a close at the same time. What about those saved during the seven years of God's wrath? Those tribulation saints are destined for an eternity with God as part of His great family. But they are not part of the bride of Christ (Revelation 7:13-17). That is in no way a knock on them. It's just a matter of timing and categorization.

The same is true when it comes to the Jews at the end of the tribulation. Israel does not become the church, and the church does not become Israel. That has to wait until a later time with the new heavens and the new earth, when there is no more sun or moon or stars. Because Israel and the church don't merge, we shouldn't expect all modalities of worship to merge either. Part of the spiritual DNA of the Jewish people is the sacrificial system, and it has been for thousands of years. For the people of Israel, offering sacrifices in the temple, when done with a humble heart and eyes focused on the Lord, is an act of glorifying God.

"But, Amir, you are skirting the issue! The Lord clearly says that sacrifices for *sin* need to be made." Patience, I'm getting there. First, we know that "without the shedding of blood there is no forgiveness of sins" (Hebrews 9:22 ESV). But what blood brings that forgiveness? Can the blood of a cow or a sheep bring true forgiveness? No, not now and not ever.

When a sacrifice was made for sin under the Mosaic law, the offense was not forgiven. It was atoned for. *Atonement* means "covering over" as opposed to "removal." Only the blood of Jesus can remove sin and bring true forgiveness. "Christ also suffered once for sins, the just for the unjust, that He might bring us to God" (1 Peter 3:18). This is the crux of the whole issue. When a person under the Mosaic law offered their sacrifice, it was covered over until the time when Jesus' blood forgave it. Animal sacrifice was a present action that looked forward to a future result.

For the believing Jews of the millennium, the timeline is reversed from that of the Mosaic law. In that upcoming era, sacrifices will look backward with the understanding that the price has already been paid. In other words, they will serve as a tangible action that reminds us of the sufficiency of the work Christ has already accomplished.

Still a little confused? Think of it like this. In the church, we celebrate communion. It is a church-based reminder, instituted by the Son of God, of the sacrifice of Jesus on the cross and the resulting forgiveness of sins. Israel is not part of the church. The Jewish people have their own traditions. The temple sacrifice hearkens back to the time of the Passover, when one lamb was killed for the life of others. That Passover sacrifice, instituted by the Father, points directly to Christ's work on the cross. In the millennium, the saved people of Israel will recognize the Passover's true meaning, which will bring a whole new level of depth to the annual sacrifice.

Thus, during the millennium, the sacrificial system will not be instituted to garner forgiveness for sins. It will serve as a worshipful reminder of the once-for-all work that Yeshua accomplished on the cross, which provided forgiveness and salvation to us as a free gift.

Final Issue #2—What's Up with the Prince?

In the midst of all the sacrificing and templing and atoning, we are faced with a new curiosity.

> He brought me back to the outer gate of the sanctuary which faces toward the east, but it was shut. And the

LORD said to me, "This gate shall be shut; it shall not be opened, and no man shall enter by it, because the LORD God of Israel has entered by it; therefore it shall be shut. As for the prince, because he is the prince, he may sit in it to eat bread before the LORD; he shall enter by way of the vestibule of the gateway, and go out the same way" (Ezekiel 44:1-3).

We've got the Lord, we've got Ezekiel, we've got the people, and we've got the priests. All are very easy to identify. But who is this mysterious prince? Maybe before we can identify him, we need to learn more about him. We've got a number of clues in Ezekiel. The first two are found in the passage above. This prince is the only one who can sit inside the Eastern Gate and eat in the presence of the Lord. Also, we see that only he is allowed to enter through the gate's vestibule and go out the same way. The rest of the people don't have that option.

But when the people of the land come before the LORD on the appointed feast days, whoever enters by way of the north gate to worship shall go out by way of the south gate; and whoever enters by way of the south gate shall go out by way of the north gate. He shall not return by way of the gate through which he came, but shall go out through the opposite gate (46:9).

As far as duties, the prince is tasked with preparing the offerings for the festivals, the new moons, and the Sabbaths with the purpose of making atonement for the people (45:17). But not only is he providing regular offerings, "the prince shall prepare for himself and for all the people of the land a bull for a sin offering" (verse 22). So the prince needs a sin offering? That throws a twist into the equation.

Finally, we see that when this prince wants to provide an inheritance for his sons, he needs to do so from his own property. He can't just confiscate other people's land, then give it to one of his kids. What land does the prince possess? It stretches from the Mediterranean to the Jordan between the newly divvied-out tribal borders of Judah and Benjamin. Part of the prince's land is dedicated to the great sacred area set aside for the temple we spoke of earlier. That all may seem like innocuous information until it hits you. "Wait, this prince has a family?"

Most evangelical commentators say that this prince is likely one of two people. There are those who hold that he is Jesus, and there are others who say that he is David. As I was speaking to my writing partner, Dr. Rick Yohn, he admitted that he had always believed that the prince was David until he started studying deeply for this book. Now he realizes that both those go-to options are impossibilities.

It cannot be Jesus. He is perfect and therefore would never need to offer a sacrifice for His sins. In fact, He was the unblemished sacrifice for everyone else's sin. Also, there were never any Yeshua Jrs. running around.

But what about David? He certainly had his share of sin in his lifetime, despite being a man after God's own heart. But that was then and this is now. In the millennium, David will be living in a resurrected state. He was buried in a natural body but raised at the Messiah's return in a spiritual body. Sin will be a thing of the past. That goes for having sons too. As much as he had a wandering eye back in his old kingdom, those fleshly days of procreation will be behind him.

So who is this prince? Once again, we don't know for sure. God determined that it was important for us to know that there would be a prince. His identity, though, was not need-to-know. My thinking is that this prince is a Jew of the tribe of Judah from the line of David who survives the tribulation. Because of his lineage, he will be given a place of authority and honor within the kingdom. He will be the corruptible flesh representative of the regency that will be headed by incorruptible King David, who will be sitting on the throne in Jerusalem. That's my *thinking*, which, as I've made clear throughout this book, is very different from my *knowing*.

Final Issue #3—Cool, Clean Water

As a tour guide for many years, a regular highlight I'd provide for pilgrims from all parts of the world was the opportunity to float in the Dead Sea. Located at the lowest point on earth (430 meters, or 1,410 feet below sea level), this body of water is composed of more than 30 percent salt. Because of its incredibly high salinity, there is no plant or fish that can survive in its waters. Thus, the name Dead Sea. There is one benefit to the water's density, and that is everyone can float. And floating on that briny water is an experience that everyone needs to have at least once. Just make sure you pack your soap.

After showing Ezekiel the temple's kitchen area, the prophet's tour guide took him back to the front of the temple. There, they found water streaming east from the right side of the structure. It wasn't deep, but its flow was steady. Before the prophet had time to ask where this water was coming from, the man led him forward. Quick cubitology note: 1,000 cubits is about one-third of a mile or a little over half a kilometer.

> When the man went out to the east with the line in his hand, he measured one thousand cubits, and he brought me through the waters; the water came up to my ankles. Again he measured one thousand and brought me through the waters; the water came up to my knees. Again he measured one thousand and brought me through; the water came up to my waist. Again he measured one thousand, and it was a river that I could not cross; for the water was too deep, water in which one must swim, a river that could

not be crossed. He said to me, "Son of man, have you seen this?" Then he brought me and returned me to the bank of the river (47:3-6).

This passage has always brought a smile to my face. I picture one of Jerusalem's hot summer days with Ezekiel sweating as he followed his guide. With each succeeding interval, the water grew deeper and he was able to feel more refreshed. Finally, he came to a place where he could wade through the water and dunk his head under the cool, clear flow that streamed from under the temple of God. I can picture the prophet laughing as he shook the water from his head, maybe getting a glare from his companion, who was wiping the droplets from his measuring line.

Ezekiel's book isn't the only place where we read about a river flowing from the temple. Not many decades after his vision, Zechariah would see something similar. Speaking of the day when Yeshua returns to the Mount of Olives, the prophet said, "The Mount of Olives shall be split in two, from east to west, making a very large valley; half of the mountain shall move toward the north and half of it toward the south" (Zechariah 14:4). We've already spoken earlier of this great earthquake. What we didn't see then was that out of the gap formed by the quake, "living waters shall flow from Jerusalem, half of them toward the eastern sea and half of them toward the western sea; in both summer and winter it shall occur" (verse 8). So half will pour down the hills of Jerusalem, west toward the Mediterranean. But where is this other half that Ezekiel is following bound for?

This easterly rushing river will follow a course that will take it all the way to the Dead Sea. Once there, rather than the bad water polluting this flow of good water, this fresh, new water will bring life to a sea that has for millennia been stone-cold dead. Ezekiel's guide said to him:

> This water flows toward the eastern region, goes down into the valley, and enters the sea. When it reaches the sea, its waters are healed. And it shall be that every living thing that moves, wherever the rivers go, will live. There will be a very great multitude of fish, because these waters go there; for they will be healed, and everything will live wherever the river goes. It shall be that fishermen will stand by it from En Gedi to En Eglaim; they will be places for spreading their nets (Ezekiel 47:8-10).

Fishermen along the Dead Sea! If you saw that today, you would think those people with the nets were insane. But the day is coming when the shores will be teeming with folks looking to catch their supper from the lake's sweet waters. Not only will there be fish in the water, but the areas surrounding the water that are now barren salt flats will be filled with fruit and herb trees with their production on hyperdrive.

> Along the bank of the river, on this side and that, will grow all kinds of trees used for food; their leaves will not wither, and their fruit will not fail. They will bear fruit every month, because their water flows from the sanctuary. Their fruit will be for food, and their leaves for medicine (verse 12).

Sometimes when I'm down by the Dead Sea, I try to envision what this will look like. But it's pretty difficult. Although there are areas where inventive farmers have managed to create some productive groves through technology, it is far from a lush area. But someday, all that will change. I do find it amusing that the area that currently houses most of the resorts will be part of the one-third of the sea that will continue to remain marshland and salt flats.

This death-to-life story is illustrative of the revitalization of the world that will take place during the millennial reign of Christ. It is also a picture of what takes place in our own hearts when we give our lives to Yeshua the Messiah.

Final Issue #4—The Abrahamic Covenant

That's right, we're back to the covenants. And this time, hold on to your hats because it's about to get awesome!

Each of the four covenants has been dealt with in Ezekiel. The conditional Mosaic covenant promised blessing with obedience and discipline with disobedience. Much of Ezekiel's book has dealt with God's correction of Israel. In the Davidic covenant, God promised the king that there would be someone from his line always on the throne. As we approached the end of Ezekiel's writings, we learned that it would be David himself. "I will establish one shepherd over them, and he shall feed them—My servant David. He shall feed them and be their shepherd" (34:23).

The new covenant is seen in the promise of a fresh relationship with the entire nation of Israel, as promised by Jeremiah.

> This is the covenant that I will make with the house of Israel after those days, says the LORD: I will put My law in their minds, and write it on their hearts; and I will be their God, and they shall be My people (Jeremiah 31:33).

In Ezekiel, this covenant of peace is played out:

> Moreover I will make a covenant of peace with them, and it shall be an everlasting covenant with them; I will establish them and multiply them, and I will set My sanctuary in their midst forevermore. My tabernacle also shall be with them; indeed I will be their God, and they shall be My people (Ezekiel 37:26-27).

Mosaic, Davidic, and new. But there is one more covenant, the foundational Abrahamic. And that is what the final chapter of Ezekiel is all about. I admit, at first glance, all the tribes and cubits and gates can seem like a bit of a dud ending to a fascinating book. But don't give up now after you've come so far. Remember, context is king. And the context here moves us to step back and look at the entire history of Israel.

In the Abrahamic covenant, God made a promise of people, blessing, and land. What land?

> To your descendants I have given this land, from the river of Egypt to the great river, the River Euphrates—the Kenites, the Kenezzites, the Kadmonites, the Hittites, the Perizzites, the Rephaim, the Amorites, the Canaanites, the Girgashites, and the Jebusites (Genesis 15:18-21).

That is a wide stretch of property. Never has Israel controlled that much area. In Solomon's heyday, Israel's borders reached their zenith, but they still didn't reach the full extent of God's promise. That is what Ezekiel 48 is all about.

The first 29 verses of this final chapter are all about reapportioning the land to the 12 tribes of Israel. In the north is Dan's portion, which reaches into Lebanon past Tyre and Sidon and into Syria beyond Damascus. Then the tribes stairstep downward until you get to Gad in the southern part of a revitalized Negev. One unified Israel, as predicted by Ezekiel's reunited branch, sharing the full amount of God's Promised Land.

Toward the middle of the nation is Jerusalem. It is the home of the temple, whose hallowed grounds, along with the portion designated to the prince, stretch from the Mediterranean to the Jordan. Flowing through that east-to-west belt will be the new river from the temple, which will reach to the Dead Sea and the Mediterranean.

Abraham has become a great nation, both physically and spiritually. The whole world has been blessed through him and his progeny. And, finally, after all these years, Israel is fully settled throughout the entire land of promise.

God's goal throughout Ezekiel was to let both His peoples and the surrounding nations know who He is. "Then they shall know that I am the Lord." He declared that over and over and over again. Undoubtedly, He accomplished His goal. We found a God who is all-powerful and who can control empires with His hands. But we also found a caring Father who passionately loves His children, and whose heart is broken when the ones He has blessed so much run off to commit adultery with other gods. Yet He never gave up on them, just like He never gives up on any who are His.

The Lord instituted a plan to draw Israel back to Himself, and you and I are in the generation in which we are blessed to watch it play out. Eventually, all Israel will recognize Yeshua as the true Messiah and will find salvation in Him. If, in the millennium, the children of Israel begin to lose sight of God again, it won't be hard to track Him down. Along with Jerusalem's facelift, the city is getting a new name.

> The name of [Jerusalem] from that day shall be:
> THE LORD IS THERE (Ezekiel 48:35).

NOTES

1. Tony Evans, *The Tony Evans Bible Commentary* (Nashville, TN: Holman Bible Publishers, 2019), 728.

2. Charles H. Dyer, "Ezekiel," in *The Bible Knowledge Commentary: An Exposition of the Scriptures*, Vol. 1, eds. J.F. Walvoord and Roy B. Zuck (Colorado Springs, CO: Victor Books, 1985), 1236.

3. "Imminent," *Merriam-Webster.com*, https://www.merriam-webster.com/dictionary/imminent#:~:text=%3A%20ready%20to%20take%20place%20%3A%20happening%20soon.

4. Dyer, "Ezekiel," 1277.

5. "Lord Acton Quote Archive," *Acton Institute*, https://www.acton.org/research/lord-acton-quote-archive.

6. "Ezekiel," 1283.

7. Stated by Winston Churchill during a radio address about the invasion of Poland; see "Quotes," *International Churchill Society*, https://winstonchurchill.org/resources/quotes/.

8. *World Happiness Report*, https://data.worldhappiness.report/table?_gl=1*1v2l5u1*_gcl_au*OTA0NzE0MjMxLjE3NDI4NDAyMDE.

9. Mark Twain, *The Innocents Abroad* (Function), Kindle edition, Chapter LVI, Location 7077.

10. "The 'Final Solution': Göring Commission to Heydrich," *Jewish Virtual Library*, https://www.jewishvirtuallibrary.org/gring-commission-to-heydrich.

11. "Wannsee Conference and the 'Final Solution,'" *Holocaust Encyclopedia*, https://encyclopedia.ushmm.org/content/en/article/wannsee-conference-and-the-final-solution.

12. "2024 UNGA Resolutions on Israel vs. Rest of the World," *UNWatch*, November 3, 2024, https://unwatch.org/2024-unga-resolutions-on-israel-vs-rest-of-the-world/.

13. If you're not familiar with Nir Tavor, you can find out more by checking out the Nir Tavor Mossad Thriller series I write with my good friend Steve Yohn.

14. "United States Population," *worldometer*, https://www.worldometers.info/world-population/us-population/.

15. "United States Coronavirus Cases," *worldometer*, https://www.worldometers.info/coronavirus/country/us/.

16. John F. Walvoord, *Every Prophecy of the Bible: Clear Explanations for Uncertain Times* (Colorado Springs, CO: David C. Cook, 2024), 176.

17. "Ezekiel 40:5," *Bible Gateway*, https://www.biblegateway.com/passage/?search=Ezekiel%2040%3A5&version=NLT.

OTHER GREAT HARVEST HOUSE BOOKS BY AMIR TSARFATI

This companion workbook to *Exploring Ezekiel* invites you to explore the themes of God's authority and faithfulness in greater detail and equips you to remain faithful until the end.

Bestselling author Amir Tsarfati reveals how Daniel's prophecies—and his unwavering faith amid a contentious culture—provide vital insights for living out these last days with hope and wisdom.

The *Discovering Daniel Workbook* will help you apply the remarkable insights of Daniel to your daily life, emboldening you to live with hope and confidence.

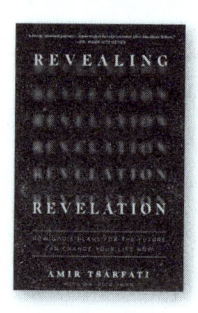

Amir Tsarfati, with Dr. Rick Yohn, examines what Revelation makes known about the end times and beyond. Guided by accessible teaching that lets Scripture speak for itself, you'll see what lies ahead for every person in the end times—either in heaven or on earth. *Are you ready?*

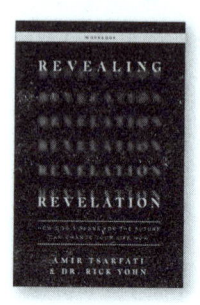

This companion workbook to *Revealing Revelation*—the product of many years of careful research—offers you a clear and exciting overview of God's perfect plan for the future. Inside you'll find principles from the Bible that equip you to better interpret the end-times signs, as well as insights about how Bible prophecy is relevant to your life today.

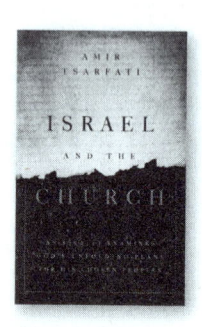

In *Israel and the Church,* bestselling author and native Israeli Amir Tsarfati helps readers recognize the distinct contemporary and future roles of both the Jewish people and the church, and how together they reveal the character of God and His perfect plan of salvation.

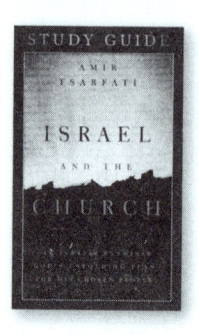

To fully grasp what God has in store for the future, it's vital to understand His promises to Israel. The *Israel and the Church Study Guide* will help you do exactly that, equipping you to explore the Bible's many revelations about what is yet to come.

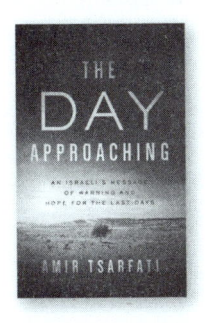

As a native Israeli of Jewish roots, Amir Tsarfati provides a distinct perspective that weaves biblical history, current events, and Bible prophecy together to shine light on the mysteries about the end times. In *The Day Approaching*, he points to the scriptural evidence that the return of the Lord is imminent.

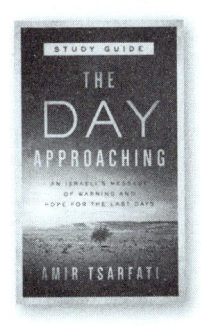

Jesus Himself revealed the signs that will alert us to the nearness of His return. In *The Day Approaching Study Guide*, you'll have the opportunity to take an up-close look at what those signs are, as well as God's overarching plans for the future, and how those plans affect you today.

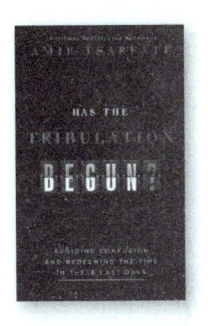

Bestselling author and native Israeli Amir Tsarfati provides clarity on what will happen during the tribulation and explains its place in God's timeline.

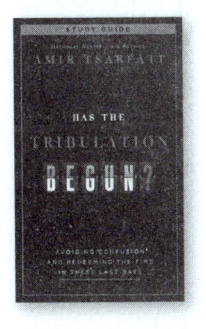

With this study guide companion to *Has the Tribulation Begun?*, bestselling author and prophecy expert Amir Tsarfati guides you through a biblical overview of the last days, with thought-provoking study and application questions.

AMIR TSARFATI WITH BARRY STAGNER

BIBLE PROPHECY: The ESSENTIALS

ANSWERS TO YOUR MOST COMMON QUESTIONS

AMIR TSARFATI & BARRY STAGNER

In *Bible Prophecy: The Essentials*, Amir and Barry team up to answer 70 of their most commonly asked questions, which focus on seven foundational themes of Bible prophecy: Israel, the church, the rapture, the tribulation, the millennium, the Great White Throne judgment, and heaven.

AMIR TSARFATI WITH STEVE YOHN

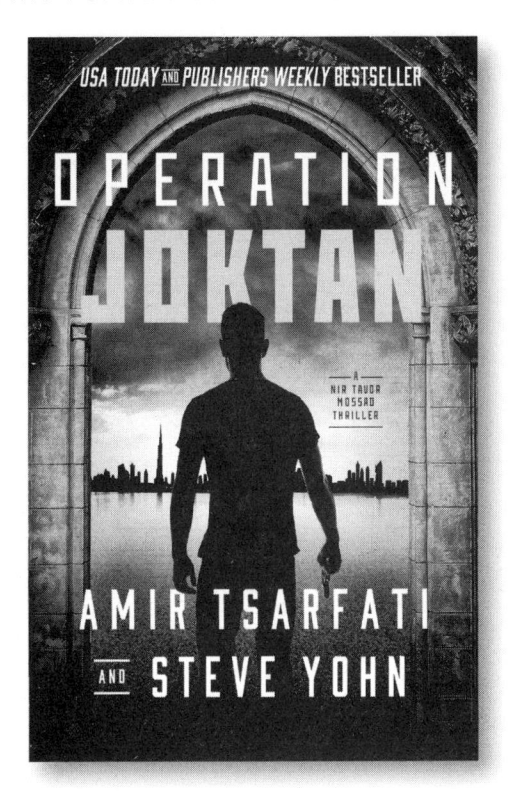

Book 1

In this first book in the Nir Tavor Mossad Thriller series, authors Amir Tsarfati and Steve Yohn draw on true events as well as tactical insights Amir learned from his time in the Israel Defense Forces. For believers in God's life-changing promises, *Operation Joktan* is a suspense-filled page-turner that illuminates the blessing Israel is to the world.

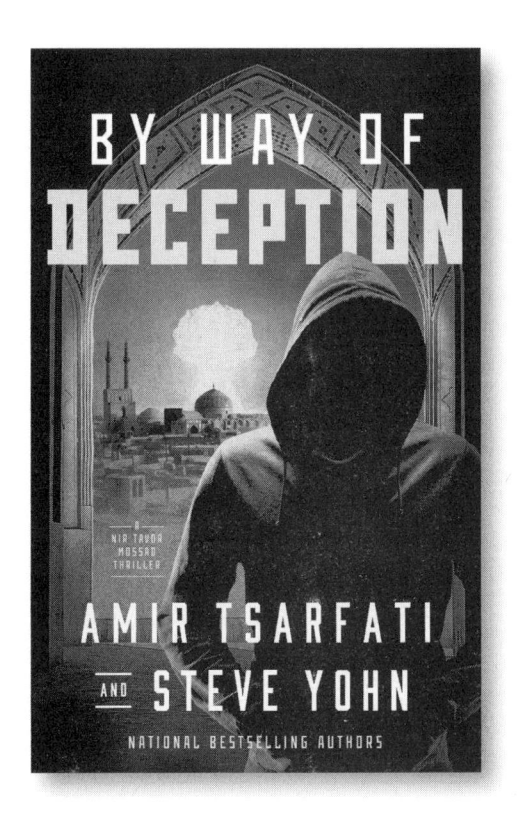

Book 2

Inspired by real events, authors Amir Tsarfati and Steve Yohn reteam for this suspenseful follow-up to the bestselling *Operation Joktan*. Filled with danger, romance, and international intrigue, this Nir Tavor thriller reveals breathtaking true insights into the lives and duties of Mossad agents—and delivers a story that will have you on the edge of your seat.

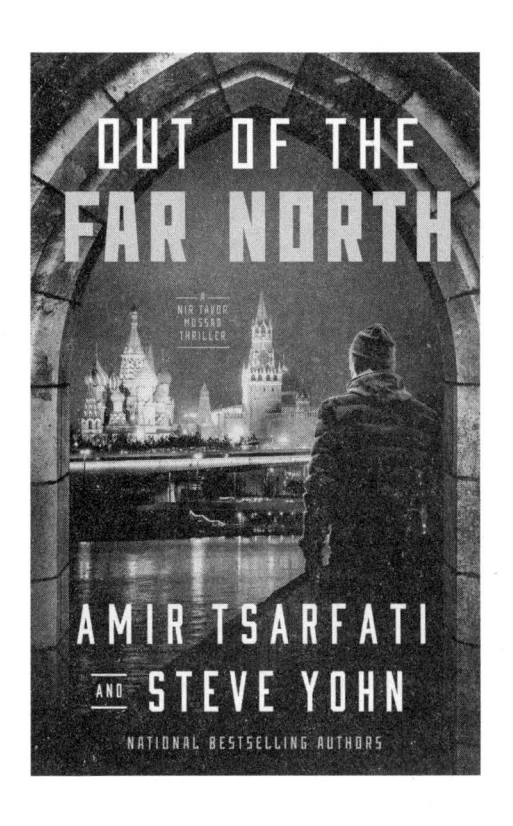

Book 3

Israel discovers that Russia is secretly planning an attack against it—but has no idea when and how. In the race to prevent a devastating conflict, will Mossad agents Nir Tavor and Nicole le Roux be able to outwit their enemies—or will their actions have catastrophic consequences?

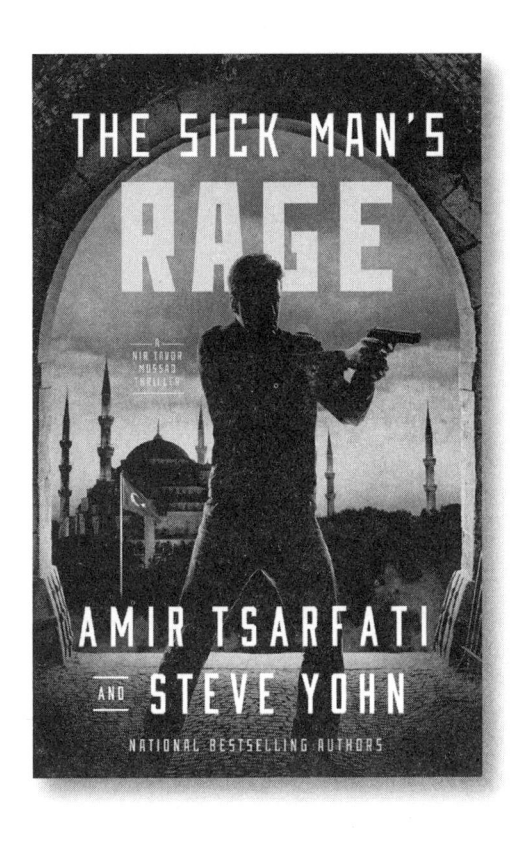

Book 4

With Israel's energy future at stake and deadly adversaries uniting against the country, Nir and his team face their most dangerous battle for survival against forces determined to see the Jewish nation fall.

BEHOLD ISRAEL

Behold Israel is a nonprofit organization founded and led by native Israeli Amir Tsarfati. Its mission is to provide reliable and accurate reporting on developments in Israel and the surrounding region.

Through Behold Israel's website, free app, social media, and teachings in multiple languages, the ministry reaches communities worldwide.

Amir's on-location teachings explain Israel's central role in the Bible and present the truth about current events amidst global media bias against Israel.

FOLLOW US ON SOCIAL

@beholdisrael

BEHOLDISRAEL.ORG

To learn more about our Harvest Prophecy resources, please visit:
www.HarvestProphecyHQ.com

HARVEST PROPHECY
AN IMPRINT OF HARVEST HOUSE PUBLISHERS